Jonas Brothers Forever

THE UNOFFICIAL STORY OF KEVIN, JOE & NICK

ECW PRESS

Copyright © ECW Press, 2009
Published by ECW Press, 2120 Queen Street East, Suite 200, Toronto, Ontario, Canada M4E 1E2
416.694.3348 / info@ecwpress.com

Jonas Brothers Forever: The Unofficial Story of Kevin, Joe & Nick is not authorized or endorsed by the Jonas Brothers, their management, Hollywood Records, the Disney Channel or the Disney–ABC Television Group. *Camp Rock* and its characters are all copyright Disney.

LIBRARY AND ARCHIVES CANADA CATALOGUING IN PUBLICATION

Janic, Susan
Jonas Brothers forever : the unofficial story of Kevin, Joe and Nick / Susan Janic.

ISBN 978-1-55022-851-9

1. Jonas Brothers (Musical group)—Juvenile literature.
2. Rock musicians—United States—Biography—Juvenile literature. I. Title.

ML3930.J765J33 2009   J782.42166092'2   C2008-907552-8

Editor: Crissy Boylan
Design and production: Tania Craan
Printing: Transcontinental

The publication of *Jonas Brothers Forever* has been generously supported by the OMDC Book Fund,
an initiative of the Ontario Media Development Corporation, and by the Government of Canada through
the Book Publishing Industry Development Program (BPIDP).

Canadä

Cover Images Copyright: Brendan Hoffman/Getty Images Entertainment (top), Frank Micelotta/Getty Images Entertainment (bottom), and Michael Williams/startraksphoto.com (back). *Interior Photos Copyright*: Carmen Portelli/Retna Ltd.: 5, 13; Brian Ach/WireImage: 6; Clark Samuels/startraksphoto.com: 7; Rena Durham/Retna: 9, 53, 55; Albert Michael/startraksphoto.com: 10; Shelby Casanova: 11, 21–23, 26–28, 30 (bottom), 31, 34, 35, 40, 41, 43, 47, 50, 52, 63, 70, 80, 84–86, 92 (bottom), 94 (bottom right), 95, 115, 121, 124, 125, 145 (right), 146, 147, 152; Alex Oliveira/startraksphoto.com: 12, 14, 19, 20; Dalle/Shooting Star: 16; Linda Lenzi/Retna/Keystone Press: 17; Kevin Parry/WireImage: 18, 59; Shaunae Perry: 24, 33, 37, 92 (top), 93, 94 (top, bottom left), 99, 100, 102, 103, 126–131, 159; Sthanlee Mirador/Shooting Star: 25, 46; Michael Simon/startraksphoto.com: 29, 57; AP Photo/Peter Kramer: 30 (top), 150; Bob Smith/Agency Photos: 32, 133, 135; AP Photo/Jennifer Graylock: 38, 91, 148; Stephen Lovekin/WireImage: 44; AP Photo/Jason DeCrow: 45; Frazer Harrison/Getty Images Entertainment: 49; Gary Gershoff/WireImage: 51; AP Photo/Reinhold Matay: 56; Pseudo Image/Shooting Star: 58, 67, 97, 111; Michael Williams/startraksphoto.co: 61, 144; ML/Agency Photos: 62, 98, 101, 104; Christine Urbina: 64, 65; Clark Samuels/startraksphoto.com: 68, 71, 72, 75, 81; Gene Duncan/startraksphoto.com: 69; Kevin Mazur/WireImage: 77, 90; Michael Simon/startraksphoto.com: 79; AP Photo/Chris Pizzello: 82, 107, 113; AP Photo/Matt Sayles: 83, 142, 158; Dave Hogan/Getty Images Entertainment: 87; AP Photo/Evan Agostini: 89, 123; Ferdaus Shamim/WireImage: 96; AP Photo/Brian Zak/Sipa Press: 106, 108; AP Photo/Litboy: 116; Pegasus/Splash News/Keystone Press: 117; Brian Prahl/Splash News/Keystone Press: 118; James Devaney/WireImage: 122; Clint Brewer/Splash News/Keystone Press: 132; Scott Burton/WireImage: 134; Sandy Huffaker/Getty Images Entertainment: 136; Erin Nicole Smith: 137, 139; AP Photo/Tammie Arroyo: 143; Paul Drinkwater/NBCU Photo Bank via AP Images: 145 (left); AP Photo/Disney World, Mark Ashman: 149; AP Photo/Matt Stroshane, Disney Channel: 151; George Pimentel/WireImage: 153; Mark Mainz/AP Images for Fox: 154; AP Photo/Jacquelyn Martin: 155; AP Photo/Matt York: 157.

PRINTED AND BOUND IN CANADA

Table of Contents

INTRODUCTION

"The Jonas Brothers are an unstoppable force that has exploded onto the music scene." Those were the words of Disney Channel's worldwide entertainment president Gary Marsh when the network announced the Jonas Brothers' reality series, *Living the Dream*, which was filmed around their summer 2008 Look Me in the Eyes tour.

Marsh was proving himself to be a master of understatement, as the ferocity and speed at which the Jonas phenomenon has taken over America is often and aptly compared to the wave of Beatlemania that swept over the country back in the early 1960s. The Jonas Brothers' success story is nothing short of astounding considering that as recently as January 2007 they were a band without a label. Their first album, *It's About Time*, failed to make much of a splash in the marketplace, ultimately resulting in their label, Columbia Records — which was undergoing management shifts at the time — "allowing" Kevin, Joe and Nick Jonas to seek their stardom elsewhere. Disney couldn't believe its luck and immediately engaged the trio to perform the song "Kids of the Future" for its 2007 CG-animated film *Meet the Robinsons*, signed them to Hollywood Records and made them part of the Mouse House hit factory.

The Jonas Brothers were in good hands, and they knew it. But they probably had no idea just how incredible their journey from there to here would be.

Over the past four years, the trio has seen their star rise from obscurity to a near-global phenomena. Their image (by all accounts an accurate reflection of who they are) is that of good, moral people who are pursuing their life passion and achieving their goals *without* sacrificing their deeply religious beliefs. They've proven themselves to be effective role models who have remained extremely down to earth despite the fact that they have become millionaires and people chant their names everywhere they go.

And the best thing about it? They *deserve* the success they've achieved. Their music — as represented by their albums *It's About Time*, *Jonas Brothers* and *A Little Bit Longer* — is terrific pop/rock, which they write and perform themselves. They pour their hearts and souls into their concerts, an approach they've taken all along whether playing to audiences of 50 or 50,000. They have a genuine appreciation for all they have achieved, and take none of it for granted. And that is a welcome change of pace from some of their industry peers.

Jonas Brothers Forever is a heartfelt tribute to three young men who have proven that any dream is within reach if you're willing to work for it.

Chapter 1

You Gotta Believe

Faith is and always has been a significant part of the Jonas family, beginning with parents Pastor Paul Kevin Jonas Sr. and his wife, Denise, who have devoted a large part of their lives to their Christian beliefs. As Denise explained after Kevin Jr., Joe and Nick started to achieve some success, "All their lives, our kids traveled with us doing Christian songs and drama in churches and open-air concerts around the country and overseas."

When Kevin Sr. and Denise were first married in the 1980s, they settled down in Teaneck, New Jersey, where they traveled from church to church, using music as an integral tool to spread the word.

They were tireless in their efforts, though good news caused the couple to slow down a bit at the beginning of 1987 when they learned that Denise was pregnant.

"I'm gonna watch you shine, gonna watch you grow, gonna paint the signs so you'll always know! I will love you forever — from dad to sons." *(from Kevin Sr.'s MySpace profile)*

Their travels didn't come to a complete stop until shortly before Paul Kevin Jonas Jr. was born on November 5.

Shortly after Kevin's birth, the family hit the road again, using "the word" as their calling card. Some time shortly after Kevin's first birthday, Denise found herself pregnant again, though travel continued until August 15, 1989, in Arizona, when she gave birth to son number two, Joseph Adam Jonas.

Now with two children to raise, Kevin Sr. and Denise decided that the time had come for them to settle down for a while — in Dallas, Texas. And it was there on September 16, 1992, that the growing Jonas family welcomed third son Nicholas Jerry.

Helping the family get used to a less travel intensive lifestyle was Kevin Sr.'s appointment as a religious leader for Christ For The Nations Institute, which describes

> **Our father is an amazing musician and singer.**

itself as "an international, interdenominational organization that exists to train and equip men and women with the Word of God in the power of the Holy Spirit . . . We seek to expand the Kingdom of God worldwide by providing resources for the completion of church buildings, caring for orphans, supporting the nation of Israel, humanitarian relief efforts, establishing and strengthening international Bible schools and the distribution of Christian literature."

The institute also had an extremely strong devotion to music, through its subsidiary Christ For The Nations Music; Kevin Sr. not only taught students theology, but also the art of creating Christian music. It served as an opportunity for Kevin Sr. to improve his own musical prowess, including his songwriting ability. As his son Kevin explained: "Our father is an amazing musician and singer. He's the kind of person who can pick up any instrument and within a few minutes he'll be playing a tune on it."

Music became so important to Kevin Sr. that by 1994 he was the president of the Christian Songwriters Association, as well as the director of Christian Faith Network Music, a division of Christ For The Nations Institute. That year he gave an interview to the *Dallas Morning News* in which he discussed the virtue of what they were attempting to do, and how it differed from the usual practice of aspiring artists bringing demos to Nashville in the hope of being discovered.

"There are songwriters in every gas station in Nashville," he said. "The world's views and the normal approach to songwriting is to try to get your song out to as many people as possible. The byproduct of this mentality is that you strive for a certain position. Our focus is on being faithful wherever we are. And if God blesses that, He will bring about the exposure in His time." Kevin Sr. passed this approach down to his sons once they were ready to pursue a career in the music industry.

Chapter 2

Growing Up Jonas

We were each other's best friends, practically. Any chance we got, we really hung out with each other.

For young Kevin, Joe and Nick, there's no doubt that growing up around music so much had an enormous influence on them, even if they didn't realize it at the time.

The boys spent the first few years of their life in Texas, memories of which are the strongest with Kevin, the oldest. "Growing up in Dallas," he reflected, "I loved playing cowboys and Indians every single day. It's just something that I loved to do — I loved getting dressed up in the whole get-up and chasing Joe around. I was a cowboy and Joe was the Indian. Nick was more toddler age in Dallas and Joe was younger too, so I had my own friends I hung out with. Of course, we all hung out together too, because we were brothers, but we got closer as we got older. I also had one really good friend named Zack, and we hung out together every single day and we took over the world together in a sense. We just had fun and ran the place. We loved where we were living and we had so much fun."

He also has a distinct memory of his bedroom in their Texas home: "I had my own room, which was cool in itself, but I remember I had a bike rack that was connected to the ceiling, so my bike hung from the ceiling. I thought that was really cool."

As much as Joe enjoyed playing games with his big brother, he found himself obsessed with a certain purple dinosaur. "Growing up," he said, "I was a very big Barney the Dinosaur fan, *huge* fan, and I had a Barney glow-in-the-dark T-shirt. I would actually go to the closet, sit down and stare at the glow-in-the-dark Barney T-shirt. If you

couldn't find me, you'd know where I was. I also remember that Kevin talked *a lot* when we were kids. Almost too much. It was my birthday one time — and we have video-tape proof of this — and we're all having fun, I'm a smiley baby and the door swings open and it's Kevin. His curly head is by the door and he's screaming out, 'It's my birth-day party.' They said it was *my* birthday party and he started to cry. It was like, 'Who invited this guy?' It was a Barney birthday party, by the way."

On a more serious note, Joe remembers a Dallas moment concerning younger brother Nick. "I remember one time when everyone was like, 'Where's Nick? Where's Nick?'" he related. "He'd snuck over the fence and jumped into the pool and he was really young. Too young to be swimming in

a pool, which was really scary. Also, the age difference between Kevin and me is about a year-and-a-half, and between Nick and me, it's about two years. We were all really close in age and we got along really well. We were each other's best friends, practically. Any chance we got, we really hung out with each other."

Nick's memories of Dallas are less dis-tinct, with him offering: "I was really big into imaginary games where I was almost acting without anybody watching. Me and my friends would imagine we were at a certain place or a certain time. The relationship between me and my brothers was cool and is cool. We would argue, but never over any-thing big. Kind of all little things, like, 'Stop wearing my socks.'"

Chapter 3

Jersey Boys

In 1996, the family made the move from Dallas back to New Jersey and to a town called Wyckoff. Kevin Sr. accepted the position of pastor at the evangelical church, the Wyckoff Assembly of God, where he focused much of his energy on both its outreach and music programs; the family home was a gray house right next to the church.

As Kevin has detailed, as much as they look back on those days lovingly, they weren't always easy given their father's vocation, which required that he be in his office Monday through Friday from the early morning into the evening, and be available to his congregation whenever they needed him. For that reason, it was difficult for the boys to participate in group sports with their father on call virtually all the time. "But it was important to all of us," said Kevin Jr., "and we all loved being there."

It was while in Wyckoff that Kevin, Joe and especially Nick developed their love for music. Explained Kevin Jr.: "We lived in the parsonage house, which is a part of the church. The church was a wonderful place. It has a stage — an awesome stage with a full drum set and platforms. It was full of music all the time, and that's where we all learned about performing and singing. My mom also sang with us, and with my dad at church. She has a beautiful voice. Our mom and dad really helped us with our music, and this was the place we celebrated music together. There was always music and singing, and I spent years on the stage there with my dad. That's where we all started singing and playing."

The move to Wyckoff had another important influence on the Jonas boys: being so close to New York City and its world-class arts scene, a whole different world opened up to them. A new side to the boys emerged, as each of them began to showcase their innate abilities to entertain others.

According to Denise, Nick more or less set everything off when, while accompanying his mom to a beauty salon, he decided

to break into song to entertain the other customers. "The stylist was blown away," she said, "and she told me to get in touch with another customer whose child was in *Les Misérables*."

This ultimately led to the Jonas family setting up an appointment with talent manager Shirley Grant, who sensed potential in all three boys, though Nick was the genuine standout at first. But as Joe detailed: "Nick had auditions for his manager, and one day we went along with him. They asked us if we would like to audition too. We ended up doing it and right away we all got signed."

What followed was a seemingly endless stream of auditions as Kevin Sr. and Denise began taking the boys to try out for commercials, plays and more. It was something they were happy to do for their boys as long as the process didn't violate their basic principles.

"We wouldn't jeopardize our values for success," Kevin Sr. related to the media.

**My wife and I never imagined
we were raising children who would become
famous performers. We were raising our sons to
become good people, good men, and that's
what makes us the proudest of them, that
they've become such wonderful people.**

"Showbiz is not that much of a priority. I'm comfortable with it going on as long as they're having fun, as long as the influences around them are not undermining our core values, but if they stopped today they'd be okay. You have to understand: my wife and I never imagined we were raising children who would become famous performers. We were raising our sons to become good people, good men, and that's what makes us the proudest of them, that they've become such wonderful people."

While lots of kids love to perform, not all parents are like Kevin Sr. and Denise, who were so willing to support their boys in such a difficult pursuit: a career in the entertainment world. "I guess it's knowing and hoping that something would happen, and that they saw something more in their kids — in a humble manner — that said, possibly it was something that could work," Kevin Jr. mused. "Our parents have sacrificed so much, more than any parents really should. And they're amazing and we appreciate everything they've ever done for us and always will."

Chapter 4

Nick Jonas
BROADWAY BOUND

Nick was the first Jonas to decide that a life in entertainment was something he wanted to pursue, and he was intent on making it happen. Which is a little surprising considering most people's first impression of him: he's very shy.

"Nick gives the impression of being quiet," explained his father, "but what he really is, is introspective and thoughtful. Nick doesn't just say something; he doesn't just give a quick opinion or say something thoughtlessly. He always wants to make sure he's thought the matter through. When he was three years old, we called him our 30-year-old man, because he was always so serious about things. He's very outgoing, but thoughtful and reserved, and if you walked by him without getting to know him, you might think he was just shy. But there's a lot of thought going on in his brain."

As to when he first became interested in entertainment, Nick related: "I was very young. My grandma said that I was in her kitchen and I got up on the table with a turkey baster and started singing. She said, 'You can't be up on the table; you're going to hurt yourself.' I was like, 'No, I have to practice.' Growing up, I always loved to sing, and I used to put on shows in my basement. Sometimes my brothers would join, but most of the time I was just trying to get people to come downstairs to watch. I would make stages out of tables and all this stuff. It was really cool."

Audition after audition finally led to Nick being cast as Tiny Tim in the Broadway musical version of *A Christmas Carol*, the annual theatrical event. Nick appeared in the 1999 season, not only as Tiny Tim but also as Young Scrooge when the Spirit of Christmas Past shows up.

For Nick, it was an amazing experience and one that had a profound effect on him, particularly helping prepare him for what he does today. "I think the experience definitely helped me in terms of learning to connect with the crowd, though working the crowd is a whole different thing," he explained. "On Broadway you don't have to work the crowd and get them hyped up. It's more about just your character connecting

Nick as Kurt von Trapp in *The Sound of Music*.

with them as well as the music and the story itself. But with a band, you have to learn how to work the crowd, how to get them pumped up and how to have them leave saying, 'Wow!' Each one of my Broadway shows brings with it its own specific memories. *A Christmas Carol* was my first Broadway show, so there was a whole lot of

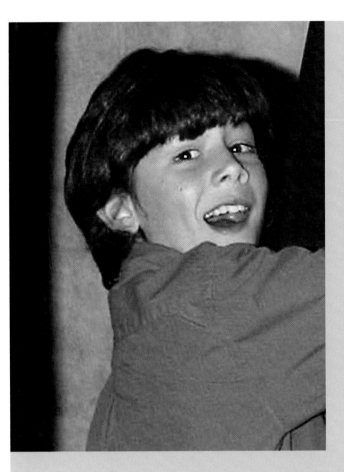

of Disney's hottest stars. "By this time," he said, "I was *really* getting accustomed to it all. I was actually there for a year, which was my longest show."

The show's producers offered Nick an extension of his run on *Beauty and the Beast* for six months, but at the same time, he had the opportunity to portray Gavroche in the long-running musical *Les Misérables*. For Nick this was something of a no-brainer: the part would be his largest to date and included a solo song. "By the time of *Les Mis*, I was totally confident about being on Broadway and it was very cool," he enthused. "I loved everything about it. It was so exciting to go on stage every day — to sing a song and know 1,500 people are watching." As Nick detailed, his being cast on the show occurred on the heels of a religious vision he had. "I was at Bible camp and I felt God saying, 'You're going to be in *Les Misérables* and touch many people.'"

Nick's next stage role was off-Broadway — way off Broadway. In New Jersey at the Paper Mill Playhouse, he portrayed Kurt von Trapp in the stage version of *The Sound of Music*, inspired by the memoir written by Maria von Trapp (played by Julie Andrews in the classic 1965 film version). Nick, who was 11 at the time, related what performing in *The Sound of Music* meant to him on a professional level: "I have this idea that when you do your fifth show, you collect your fifth point, which makes a star."

nervous energy going on." In 2000, Nick experienced another first, in his role of older brother to new arrival Frankie.

In 2001, the attention he received for *A Christmas Carol* played no small part in his being cast as Little Jake in a revival of *Annie Get Your Gun*, where he worked alongside legends like Crystal Bernard and Reba McEntire. During that show, Nick admitted, "I was still getting used to the whole Broadway thing."

Next up he was cast as the teacup Chip in the live-action Broadway version of the Disney animated classic *Beauty and the Beast*. No one could have guessed so early on in his career that years later he'd be one

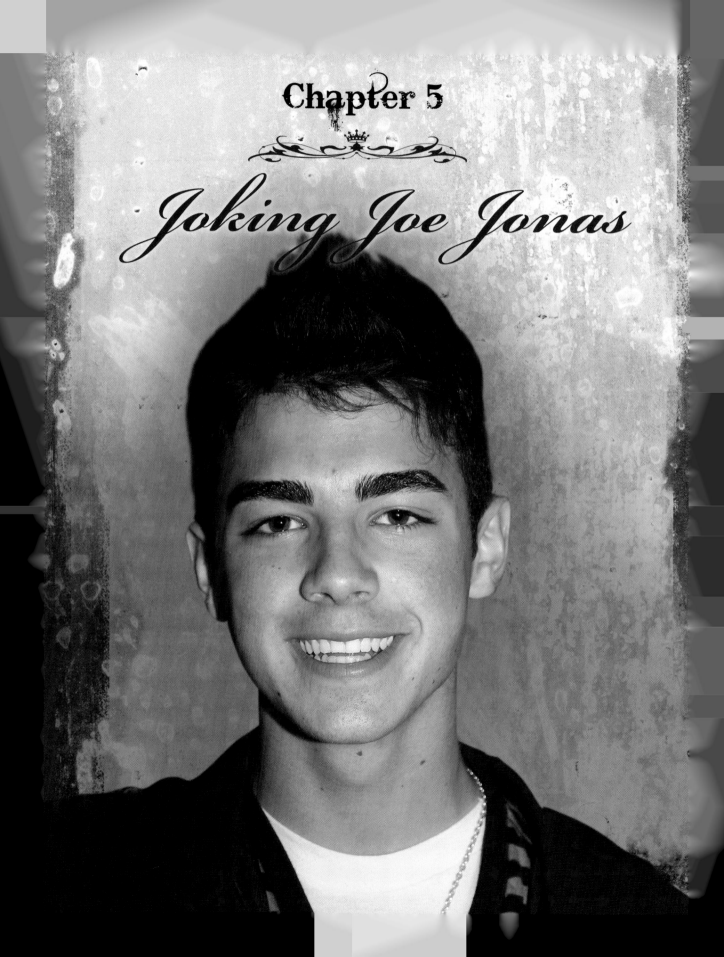

Chapter 5

Joking Joe Jonas

Making people laugh was the biggest joy for Joseph Jonas; his ambition while growing up was to become a cast member of the Nickelodeon ensemble series *All That*. Music was far off his radar. Recalled Kevin Sr.: "When Joe was younger, we had some people over and everyone was just sitting around, eating and talking. Suddenly, Joe got up and started doing this . . . I guess you could call it a comedy routine. Nick was already doing some Broadway shows and Kevin was acting in commercials, and Joe had been saying, 'I'm not interested,' but then during this family gathering, he just started performing, jumping, telling jokes, singing and dancing. Everyone in the family was amazed at what he could do. He was like this little live wire, full of energy, and you couldn't take your eyes off him. It's not surprising now that he's the band's frontman — he always knew how to grab an audience."

The way Joe remembers it, he first became interested in entertainment when he was 10 or 11 years old. "Nicholas," he said, "seemed to be singing almost from the day he was born. Everywhere he went, he sang. I just wasn't into that; I was into moviemaking. I had our home camera and I would make videos with my brother and things like that."

Which is not to say that Joe wasn't working, but he had different interests than his younger brother Nick. "Actually," he clarified, "I really did a lot of commercials and print jobs, and then I told my parents I didn't want to sing. They were like, 'Why

not, Joe?' 'I don't know' wasn't the best reason. I guess I enjoyed being a normal kid at school, but when Nick started getting some attention from some girls, I was like, 'Maybe I should try it.' I was never into sports, because I was into music more than I was sports. I started to get into musicals and that became my focus. I became a Broadway kid and wanted to dance all the time and sing. I'd walk into a grocery store and sing, 'Those are tacos!' It got worse and worse in every store I walked into. So in the beginning, all I wanted to do was make people laugh, but then I discovered that I loved singing. And it started from there: everything I say I'm not going to do, I end up doing."

Professional singing entered his life a bit unexpectedly, when he accompanied Nick to an audition for *Oliver!*, which fortunately took place shortly after Joe decided that he would start auditioning for musicals.

"Nick came to the audition at a local theater and he had a callback," Joe said. "I was in the lounge playing my video games. The door opened and there was a table full of producers and directors and Nick was standing there. He said, 'Joe, they want to see you.' I was like, 'They what?' I didn't know what was going on, but I kind of got up and walked in. I had long, shaggy hair and glasses and they were whispering to each other. They said, 'Can you please come back tomorrow?' 'Okay.' 'Thank you.' I found out they wanted Nick for the lead role of Oliver and they wanted me for the role of the Artful Dodger. From that, I came back the next day and I got it on the spot. It was one of the greatest experiences for me ever."

Ultimately Nick didn't do the show because he was cast in a Broadway show instead. But as far as Joe was concerned, *Oliver!* was "the best thing ever for me. From that point, I didn't want to do anything else. It really taught me how to perform on stage, and it helped me to come out of my shell. I was 12 or 13. The director was really hard on me, but it was something I really loved and he will always be in my book as someone who helped me to perform. He showed me you can take chances on stage. Being up there on stage, even in the rehearsals, I remember I was having a hard time performing. He was like, 'Okay,

I became
a Broadway kid
and wanted to dance all
the time and sing. I'd walk
into a grocery store
and sing.

Joe, if you don't act out and go crazy with this character, they may have to get another person.' When I heard that, I freaked out, because I was having so much fun. So the next day I decided to go crazy and he loved it. So I became the crazy kid in the cast."

There was one more stop before Joe embarked on his recording career: Baz Luhrmann's Broadway production of *La Bohème*. "The audition room was packed," Joe reflected. "I had seven callbacks over six months. Finally, the last callback was at a roller rink and we had to skate, which was real confusing. I didn't know what I was doing with the roller skates, but my dad knew what to do and he found me the best roller skating coach in New Jersey. For two days in a row, six hours a day, we worked so hard. First it was me trying to stand up, and by the end I was doing spins in the air. It was just crazy, and I was like, 'Thank you, God, for helping me.' I was so proud, because I ended up being the best kid there. You walk in there and you don't know what to expect. I was so happy to know that I was the only one who knew cool tricks. [The coach] taught me to look good. So I was on Broadway for eight months and it was amazing."

Chapter 6
Kevin Jonas
GUITAR HERO

Even when he was very young, Kevin Jonas Jr. revealed himself to be a very conscientious person, who sometimes seemed to make more demands of himself than anyone else did. Years later his father would observe: "Kevin is the type of person who can be very hard on himself, because he wants to do things perfectly the first time. He's such a hard worker and expects a lot from himself. We sometimes have to tell him that things are going to be fine, but he's a natural worrier. He's never going to leave a job half-done. He's going to work things through until he's got it down perfectly."

It's actually that aspect of his personality that played an integral role in Kevin's eventual evolution to lead guitarist in the Jonas Brothers. "I was home sick for a week from school with strep throat," Kevin explained. "I didn't want to watch *The Price Is Right*, I was getting tired of watching Nick Jr., which was the only thing on for kids — how many times could you watch the same episode of *Blues Clues*? — and I wasn't going to watch a soap opera and that whole, 'I love you,' 'I hate you,' 'I love you,' 'I hate you' thing. We had a copy of a 'teach yourself guitar' book and I've never put the guitar down since. Actually, I would say to myself that I never would sing, and then I ended up singing.

"I guess it just wasn't my thing — or I

thought it wasn't," he continued. "I wanted to be that kid who filmed the skateboarders; the one who wore the clothes but couldn't skate. But then Nick started getting a lot of attention from the ladies and I changed my mind."

As to that book and guitar just laying around the house, waiting for Kevin to pick them up and change his life, he explained: "We'd always been a musical family, so it was just one of those situations. My dad grew up singing in country bars, and my dad was actually a musical director at a Christian college. We grew up and lived there, and he did a big live worship tape every year. So we kind of grew up in the studio, and my dad is an amazing vocalist and piano player, and we learned a lot of our vocal part from him. He was very involved. We loved working with him, and whenever I had questions, he would help me out and teach me new things."

Although Kevin had enjoyed considerable success in TV commercials and in print advertising, that fateful time he was home sick has become the most important moment in his professional life. "That was the day I realized that I was meant to play music," he said.

Chapter 7

Frankie

THE BONUS JONAS

Frankie cracks wise on *TRL* with his older brothers and VJ Lyndsey Rodrigues in August 2008.

The one Jonas sibling who has so far avoided the spotlight (at least compared to his older brothers) is Frankie Nathaniel Jonas, who was born on September 28, 2000.

In the early days of the Jonas Brothers' career, fans spotted Frankie in family photos and as part of the background action in footage of the Jonases moving from venue to venue. So how long would it be before Frankie became both a Jonas brother and a part of the Jonas Brothers? "He said he kind

of wants to make his own band," said Nick. "He hasn't warmed up to the idea of being in our band." And Frankie followed through on that and formed his own band, Webline.

Kevin added, "He's on the road with us while we're on tour. He *loves* being on the tour bus and thinks that we should sell our house, buy a bus and forever be on a bus. You know, he never even likes to watch our concerts. He'd rather stay on the bus and play the Wii."

Fans love Frankie and he's been more and more in the spotlight as he's grown older; his older brothers even devoted an entire episode of *Living the Dream* to Frank the Tank. Whatever the future holds for the youngest Jonas, it is sure to be remarkable.

Chapter 8

Nick Flies Solo

While Nick was on Broadway playing Chip in *Beauty and the Beast*, he and his dad co-wrote a song called "Joy to the World (A Christmas Prayer)" for Broadway's annual Equity Fights AIDS disc, *Broadway's Greatest Gifts: Carols For a Cure, Volume 4*. Besides the fact that Nick and Kevin Sr. collaborated on the song, it was made extra special with background vocals by the cast of *Beauty and the Beast*.

In November 2003, a demo of the song was submitted to INO Records, part of Sony Records based in Nashville, Tennessee. The label is devoted to contemporary Christian music and describes itself as follows: "We desire to work with artists who have a unique message, excellent artistry and spiritual maturity . . . Our chief aim is to know God and make Him known through products that are spiritually significant, artistically excellent and culturally relevant."

Apparently Nick and "Joy to the World (A Christmas Prayer)" met all three criteria as INO released the song to Christian radio stations, where it enjoyed some popularity. By September 2004, with the success of the song, Nick was signed to both INO and Columbia as a solo artist. His first album was announced, and its first single, "Dear God," was released. By November a solo version of "Joy to the World (A Christmas

Prayer)" was released as well. Nick's album was slated for December, before it was delayed a number of times.

In an attempt to gain attention for his music, Nick issued a letter to Christian radio to spread the word. "Dear friend," that letter began, "I wanted to thank you for doing the work that you are doing for the Lord. Last year I had the privilege to have many Christian radio stations playing my Christmas song, 'Joy to the World (A Christmas Prayer).' It was amazing to see how many people were touched during Christmas. Christian radio allowed that song to get out there and I really appreciated it.

"This year," he continued, "I got the chance to record an actual full CD with INO and the first song we're sending out to radio is called 'Dear God.' It is a song that really impacted me and I hope will impact many others. It is a prayer to God from my heart. It talks about all of the things that are going on around the world. If we just go to the Lord, like a child, He will help us. My favorite line in the song is 'I think I see a rainbow from behind the clouds and I hear you now. Dear God.' Everybody needs to know that God is there for them.

"My goal for this record is to touch people's lives. I would love to see people come to the Lord. So many people are hurting and lost. I just hope that they find hope through this song."

At the same time, Kevin Sr. issued his own letter, which read in part, "I am writing to you as a father and pastor of Nicholas

Jonas. I know him better than anyone except the Lord. When Nicholas was a small boy, I knew that there was something special about him. He had a great voice. He possessed a dramatic talent. He was as cute as you could imagine. But the greatest thing about Nicholas was his heart. He truly loves the Lord. His talent belongs to God. His words are born in relationship to the Savior. He has a deep passion for the Lord that touches all those around him.

"Last year," he added, "so many stations played our song 'Joy to the World (A Christmas Prayer).' People from all over the nation wrote us. We heard from children, parents and grandparents. There were messages from cancer victims and child advocates. There were letters from members of the church community as well as those outside our community. Some families decided to give money to missions and ministries instead of spending it all on themselves. Each night I was able to read these letters of

encouragement to Nicholas. Christian radio was vitally important in making this happen. Much has happened over the last year. Nicholas is now signed to INO Records as a recording artist. They have partnered with Columbia Records to impact people throughout the nation. It is thrilling to see the potential."

In a press release about Nick's signing, INO Records president Jeff Moseley admitted, "I entered into the idea of working with a 12-year-old with fear and in trepidation. My fears have quickly resolved after realizing just how purposeful he is about what God has called him to do. He has an amazing sense of acuity when it comes to goals and dreams. In today's age with pre-manufactured pop, even as young as he is, Nicholas is a breath of fresh air as he has the ability to 'voice' his projects through his singing and songwriting."

For his part, Nick added, "This is my first record, so I'm very excited about this new experience and I am blessed to have a family that is so loving and supportive of what I'm doing. I hope this record touches a lot of people and I've been praying that the Lord will use it in a big way. The hope of this record is to make people feel good and happy inside. I'm excited to see what comes next."

Unfortunately, it wasn't much. The album, *Nicholas Jonas*, only received a limited release after several delays. Part of the cause for the less-than-stellar debut was newly installed Columbia Records president Steve Greenberg who heard Nick's disc

and decided he was much more a fan of the artist than the tracks on the album. Greenberg eventually met with Nick and heard the track "Please Be Mine" (written by Nick, Joe and Kevin), as did A&R executive Dave Massey.

Explained Joe: "They thought Nick had an angel-like voice, which is what got him signed. Nick had started working on his solo project and one day Kevin and I were like, 'Hey, Nick, do you think we can write a song together?' So we wrote 'Please Be Mine,' which was the first song we wrote together and it's a song the fans love. We walked into the label one day and Dave Massey freaked out and said, 'Whoa, there are brothers?' From that moment, we immediately became a group project and started working with different people every day. But Kevin and I did not expect that we were going to become a brother band at all. We thought it would be cool to maybe do a song. Maybe we could be, like, the backups once in a while, but this brother band just happened and we all went along with it."

Chapter 9

Band of Brothers

Why is it that so many successful bands are made up of family members? Is it because of shared musical genes? Is it the trust and understanding that comes from knowing your bandmates since day one? Maybe sibling rivalry drives these bands to push their boundaries and make great music. Whatever it is, there have been some great brother bands in recent years, even before the Jonas Brothers took center stage.

Hanson is the band the JoBros were most often compared to when they were starting out. Like the Jonas Brothers, Hanson got their start in their teens and won a wide fan base with their insanely catchy hit "MMMBop" back in 1997. The Jonas Brothers actually acknowledge Hanson as predecessors, and even challenged them to a dance battle in the song "That's Just the Way We Roll." Taylor Hanson admires the Jonas Brothers, saying in an interview that they will go far because, like Hanson, they stick together and write their own songs.

Brother bands are not just a recent thing either — they have been tearing up the charts for a long time. The Jackson 5 is one of the most successful sibling bands ever, while the Beach Boys and the Bee Gees also found massive success. New Kids on the Block features Jordan and Jonathan Knight, 98 Degrees had Nick and Drew Lachey, and Oasis relies on the tension between feuding brothers Noel and Liam Gallagher to give their music an edge. It's safe to say that Oasis isn't built on the same kind of brotherly love that the success of the Jonas

Brothers is — Liam once attacked Noel with a tambourine on stage, and Noel has walked out on the band several times.

There's a new generation of brother bands coming through the ranks alongside the Jonas Brothers. Alex and Nat Wolff are the stars of the Naked Brothers Band, My Chemical Romance is led by the sibling tandem of Gerard and Mikey Way, and Good Charlotte's Benji and Joel Madden are identical twins. The Kings of Leon, meanwhile, like the Jonas Brothers, are made up of three sons of a churchman. Caleb, Jared and Nathan Folowill, along with their cousin, Matthew, named their band after their father and grandfather, both of whom are called Leon.

And it's not just brothers who are making great music — sisters are doing it too. Tegan & Sara and Smoosh are storming up the charts, while The Veronicas have toured with the Jonas Brothers. These girls are following the trail blazed by earlier sister bands such as The Corrs, the Dixie Chicks and Heart.

Whatever the reason for the success of sibling bands, it's clear that they have an edge on the competition — and fans of the Jonas Brothers are grateful that the execs at Columbia saw the potential with all three brothers together. The brothers themselves realized how amazing it could be to work together. "I think the breaking point for us was when we started writing songs together," Kevin mused, "and seeing that we could do it, and loving it and having fun together. The songwriting did come naturally, it really did.

The first song we ever wrote together was the song that got us signed, so it was either luck, fate or something in between. We hit *something*."

In an interview with *Billboard*, Columbia president Greenberg explained: "I didn't like the record [Nick had] made, but his voice stuck out, so I met with him and found out he had two brothers. I liked the idea of putting together this little garage-rock band and making a record that nodded to the Ramones and '70s punk. So we went into the studio with the Jonas Brothers and did it."

Not that the rest of the world knew they'd been signed. "We did demos in a basement for weeks on end," reflected Kevin. "We

didn't tell anyone we had gotten signed, because people can freak out a little. But we started working with writers. I remember that I missed three to four days of school every single week and people were like, 'Where are you?' but I couldn't say anything, because we'd talked about keeping it to ourselves. Truthfully, it could backfire on you in a sense, and we didn't want that. My school knew the truth and they were amazing and really honored with what we were doing. They were so helpful with what we did, and we actually went back and played two sold-out nights in the school to say thanks." The school situation was remedied when the Jonas family resolved that if the boys were pursuing a career in entertainment, they would be better off home-schooled.

A Nick Jonas disc had a different sound and sensibility from one featuring all three brothers. "I think my sound was a little more adult contemporary," he said. "If I

The first song
we ever wrote together
was the song that got us signed,
so it was either luck, fate or
something in between.
We hit something.

were to release a solo record, it would probably sound a little more funky than a Jonas Brothers album, a little more R&B and soul-like. I love that kind of music and I would say that's my style."

The sound wasn't the only change: the Jonas Brothers would be making the jump from the Christian market to the mainstream. In a worst-case scenario, when a band crosses over, their Christian audience feels they have been betrayed by the band's quest for fame and glory, while their new mainstream audience remains resistant to Christian messages, leaving the band without an audience. This is a situation the Jonas Brothers avoided.

Nick, Joe and Kevin have charmed Christian and mainstream audiences alike with their disarming honesty and refusal to preach. They're upfront about their faith. "We are Christians and our faith is really important to us. It's a big thing in everything we do," the band has explained. However, the Jonas Brothers don't express their religious beliefs through their lyrics. Their Christianity comes through in more subtle ways — their purity rings, for example, which symbolize their vow not to have pre-marital sex. When Russell Brand made fun of their rings on the 2008 MTV Music Awards, Christians and non-Christians alike thought it was mean and unfair, and Brand apologized.

Some bands have not been so lucky as the JoBros. Stryper, a Christian metal band from the '80s, was one of the first to encounter the crossover problem. They were very successful, but their failure to juggle their Christian and mainstream audiences led to their downfall. When they praised God, the mainstream ridiculed them. When they changed their message and their look, their Christian audience revolted. More recently, Creed, P.O.D., Lifehouse and Switchfoot have dealt with the problem by downplaying the Christianity in their music. "For us, it's a faith, not a genre," said Switchfoot's Jon Foreman in an interview with the *Boston Globe*. "Calling us 'Christian rock' tends to be a box that closes some people out and excludes them. And that's not what we're trying to do."

In the future, bands trying to make the leap from Christian to mainstream should consider taking a page out of the Jonas Brothers' playbook.

With a new sound and a new mainstream focus, the other major change was for Nick — going from a solo act to a group member. "For a minute," he admitted, "it was a little tough, and then it was all good when I realized how cool it would be to tour and record with my brothers. And because we're brothers, there's no way to kick one of us out of the band. We've always thought about having a production company, running a record company together, doing something like that, keeping it in the family. It's awesome to have my brothers on stage and in the studio with me. You have a security that everything is going to be okay, even when you mess up."

Elaborated Kevin: "There's a support

system. It's a lot easier with us being brothers. No one's standoffish. You can't get upset with each other . . . you're a core group and you're on stage every night with each other."

"It's really cool," enthused Joe, "because when you look on stage you see Nick and not some random kid. If something happens, if something goes wrong, we know what happens. It's not like we have this huge thing afterwards, like, 'What happened? I didn't know where you guys were!' That kind of thing. You always know what's going on. We love each other to death."

The boys have related how they work together, with Kevin explaining their method of songwriting as follows: "It feels like the most natural thing we could be doing. When we write a song, we get in a triangle. I start playing the chords that we've chosen over and over and then we'll keep going around until we have figured out the lyrics for our song."

Joe added: "We approach songwriting as a group. We live together, travel together and love to write together. Everything we do we can turn into a song."

"We get our inspiration from a lot of different places," said Nick. "A lot of the songs are from personal experiences. So

things that we have gone through in the past we have been able to put into song and make it cool."

And in terms of the brothers' roles in the band, Joe said, "Nicholas is the powerhouse vocal. He's just got this young, soulful voice that catches everyone's ear."

Offered Nick: "Joseph just has this really cool, smooth rock voice. He really knows how to get the crowd going. Kevin is the one that holds us all together. Joseph and I are the singers and we take turns on keyboards and percussions, but Kevin mostly plays the guitar and that's the part of the group that we need — he's the glue that keeps it together."

Nick explained that a lot of thought went into the name of the group: "Our name at the beginning was Sons of Jonas. Then it was Jonas 3, then they thought about calling us Jonas Cubed, then Jonas, Jonas, Jonas; and Run, Jonas, Run. Finally we went on stage for our first concert and we decided that Jonas Brothers would be cooler than Jonas 3 or something like that." In all these crucial first decisions, the Jonas Brothers made the right choices.

Chapter 10

It's About Time

were and how to do it. We were definitely new to the whole music thing. The first album was a real collaborative effort between us, the writers and the A&R people at Columbia Records. We really worked to find out what our sound was."

And Columbia Records worked hard to get the word out to the world about the Jonas Brothers, a challenge they met in 2005 by arranging for the siblings to be the opening act for a number of popular performers, including Jesse McCartney, The Click Five, the Backstreet Boys, Aly & AJ, The Cheetah Girls and The Veronicas.

On the surface this all sounds pretty glamorous, but according to Kevin, it really wasn't. The experience, he points out, was worth everything they went through, but it was actually harder than any of them had imagined.

"It costs a lot to be on the road, but we've been very blessed," said Kevin. "We all know what it's like to not have a lot, so the fact is when we can bring people on, bring crew members on, it's amazing. When we were first signed to Columbia Records, we toured but it was in a van and trailer. We did opening dates, and you don't make a lot of money. They say if you want to open for Jesse McCartney or Backstreet Boys, you're not going to make anything. The exposure level is so high that it's worth it to go on those tours, but you don't make a lot of money on them."

Said Nick: "Most people don't understand how much work it really takes. You have to keep doing it every day, building up

Now signed to Columbia Records, the newly christened Jonas Brothers began working with various songwriters, although the brothers were given writing or co-writing credits on seven of the album's final 11 tracks, which in itself was a pretty amazing achievement.

"Oh, we were up for days and days," smiled Kevin. "We worked with a guy named P.J. Bianco, who was actually a friend of our father's. We started writing songs with him and other people and it was really great. We were playing a lot of instruments and were just hanging out, pulling up iTunes and listening to other songs that we'd like to consider. And there [was] a basketball court, so we played a lot. On that first album, we were trying to find out who we

your voice throughout the entire day, and then you have a show at, like, 10."

"It gets tiring," Joe admitted, "but, you know, the fact is that when you get back on stage, it's worth every bit. Every bit of energy that you spent to get there, it's completely worth it."

During those days, Kevin, Nick and Joe slept in a van while Kevin Sr. drove them throughout the night and sometimes over the course of several days to the next gig. The Jonases also served as their own crew. For instance, they went out on a school tour — performing at different schools to introduce kids to their music — which required that they wake up at three each morning to get to the designated school on time. Once there, they would unload all of their equipment and set up the PA system, accompanied by one other person. Staying at hotels was usually not an option as there was no budget to support it. "If the concert was in Boston," Kevin said, "we might stay in a hotel because it was a four-and-a-half hour trip, but with Philly we drove back after the show. And we learned how to play without sound checks, and we worked hard."

The hands-on experience taught the guys how to be roadies and while physically taxing, it was also eye-opening in terms of what professional roadies' lives are like all the time.

"It was crazy," Kevin noted of the period, "and it was also absolutely an amazing time in our lives. But now, as we have some kind of success, it's a gift from God because now

we have a crew, now we have four different guys that are always with us. Our band walks in and everything is set up and they can do their sound check, and then we walk in and we sound check as a band, then we walk off stage after an hour and we're done. And it's the greatest feeling having someone hand you a guitar. We've always been so blessed to have the opportunity to do what we do, but now we have the opportunity to also enjoy it."

But before that opportunity could come, Columbia needed to build a grassroots following to ensure the success of the band's debut disc. To this end 2006 kicked off with the label announcing the Jonas Brothers' American Club Tour.

"The Jonas Brothers, the emerging teenage powerpop garage rock band hailing from New Jersey, will hit the road in late January for a series of American club dates," Columbia Records told the media. "The Jonas Brothers' winter tour will give fans a chance to catch the boys in intimate club settings before the group's eagerly awaited debut album, *It's About Time*, hits the stores on Tuesday, April 11.

"The Jonas Brothers," Columbia continued, "have developed their own signature sound, pouring soaring vocal harmonies, unforgettable melodic hooks and boundless energy into fresh original songs, most of them written by the Jonas Brothers, with collaborators including Adam Schlesinger (Fountains of Wayne), Michael Mangini (Joss Stone), Desmond Child (Aerosmith,

Bon Jovi), Billy Mann (Jessica Simpson, Destiny's Child) and Steve Greenberg (Joss Stone, Hanson). The Grammy-winning duo of Greenberg and Mangini, fresh off their success with Joss Stone's two acclaimed albums, produced *It's About Time*, drawing on the Jonas Brothers' unpretentious garage rock sound and affinity for hooky '70s British punk records. Inspiration for the group's songs comes directly from the boys' personal experiences — from the highs and lows of dating to being on the road to having been given the opportunity to follow their dreams at such a young age. 'A lot of it is about typical teenage love stuff like, "Oh, what am I going to do if I can't see her today?" It's not stuff that we don't know about,' says Nicholas."

Each song on *It's About Time* has special meaning for Nick, Joe and Kevin, beginning with "What I Go to School For." As Nick explains it, that was a song that was originally done by the group Busted. "It's one of my favorites to play live," he pointed out, "because the crowd really gets into it, which is really cool." Elaborated Kevin, "It's about falling in love with an older girl in school and having a crush on her. Everyone in the

audience loves to be jumping up and down to it. It's a really energetic song." For his part Joe has admitted that every time they perform the song live, he dedicates it to his third grade teacher, "Because I had a really big crush on her."

"Time for Me to Fly" was among one of the first songs the trio wrote together, following "Please Be Mine." Nick called it a favorite because "it has a really good message and people really connect to it." Joe explained that the focus of the song is forgetting about your worries. "People just want to feel free sometimes," he said, "and that's what's cool about this song." Kevin believed that this was an inspirational track, and that it "changed a lot of things for us."

The song "Year 3000" was added late in the recording process, because, as Kevin explained it, "The label came back in and wanted to change a few things, and we agreed. Of course, 'Year 3000' became one of our biggest hits." Pointed out Joe, "We reworked it with an amazing producer and we had such an amazing time recording it." Added Nick, "Just a really fun song, and when we first recorded it, we were so excited about doing it." The video for the song, directed by Andrew Bennett, captured the energy and playfulness of the song with the boys traveling to the future through a magic portal in a couch.

"One Day at a Time" was, according to Nick, "about missing someone, and every day you're just waiting for the next time you'll see that person, and like the title says,

just waiting one day at a time." Added Kevin: "It's just knowing you want to be somewhere else and with someone else rather than just being bored. This reminds me of a summer with nothing to do." For Joe, "It's a love song about a teenager growing up and they do the same thing every day, but it still comes back to missing that one person they care about."

As detailed by Kevin, "6 Minutes" was a track provided to them, though "of course you want to put your own spin on the song, which happened with the production. Lyrically we wanted to make some changes, but legally weren't able to." Nick described it as a great song to play live because it has the "perfect tempo to jump to and it's just a fun song." Joe felt the track had an "old-school reggae feeling to it and it's fun to play live."

"Mandy" was pretty significant to all three Jonas Brothers. Explained Nick: "That was our first single ever as a band, and we recorded three music videos for it. Same song, but we created an ongoing storyline and there was a cliffhanger for each one." The story starts in a high school classroom with Nick picking up Mandy's phone after it falls out of her schoolbag. He follows her out to the parking lot to return it and she goes off with her boyfriend in his car. The episode ends with the boy trying to scare

Nick by speeding toward him on the road while Mandy tries to get him to quit fooling around. In the second episode, Nick gets away from the bully when his brothers show up in their convertible. On prom night, Mandy needs to get home before midnight and gets a ride with the JoBros, leaving her prom king boyfriend behind. When she gets home, her dad is really mad and she runs out of the house to find both the JoBros and her jock boyfriend waiting for her. Who will she choose? In the final episode, Mandy breaks up with her boyfriend and hangs out with Nick and Joe. The jealous ex threatens them so Mandy gets Kevin to help, and they drive off in the convertible to the JoBros concert!

Joe noted: "Mandy [VanDuyne] is one of our best friends. She grew up with us and I actually dated her, but then we broke up. But we're still best friends, which doesn't happen often." Enthused Kevin, "It's funny to play that song every night, because there really is a Mandy, and when she comes to the show, it's like she's a celebrity. The song is completely about her."

"Just Don't Know It" was co-written with Desmond Child, who, according to Kevin: "has written everything under the sun and is an excellent writer. We had a blast and it was so much fun to do!" Nick completely agreed, while Joe joked: "I call this the stalker love song. You know, the kid who always has the crush on the girl, saying, 'One day I'm going to be with you, you just don't know it.'"

Nick pointed out that "I Am What I Am" is a song that they opened every concert promoting the first album with, and one that the fans loved. Said Joe, "It's just about being comfortable with who you are and having a good time," while Kevin admitted, "Another one we actually didn't write, and when we first heard it, we didn't like it at all. But we still recorded it and somehow fell in love with it."

"Underdog" was, said Kevin, a track with an important message: "Our hope was that it would show that there's a beautiful side and something important in every single person out there, no matter who they are. No matter what you may say to them, they might be someone who can change the world." Expanded Joe, "It's about that person being the underdog, who everyone doesn't expect to one day do something great, but then they end up doing just that." Originally, according to Nick, this song was "more acoustic-guitar sounding and mellow, but we really rocked it out in production, and I think it made the song more exciting for people."

"7:05" began with Nick, who said it had a "cool piano part and we worked off that and came up with the song." While Kevin viewed it as a "good, fun pop song we wrote that was just designed to be cute and fun," Joe explained that it "talks about you seeing the girl you care about with another guy, which is kind of like, 'Ouch!' So much happens in that song."

It's About Time wrapped up with "Please Be Mine," which will always be important to the brothers. "The song that got us signed," smiled Kevin. "We still play it every night, and I hope we always will. It's a song that we really love to play because of what it did for us." Added Nick, "It really was a new beginning in all of our lives, which makes the song even more special." Joe revealed: "We were really fighting for it to be on the album, because we were working on someone else's songs on a lot of the tracks. The song was so important to us, and we're just happy it made it."

Nick, Kevin and Joe put their hearts and souls into the making of *It's About Time*, but, unfortunately, things didn't go exactly as Columbia had hoped and planned. While the boys continued to promote the album, its release date kept being pushed back. The single "Mandy" was released on December 27, 2005, but it took until February 22, 2006, for the video supporting the song to make its debut on MTV's *TRL*. That same month saw their song "Time for Me to Fly" issued as a part of the soundtrack for the motion picture *Aquamarine*. The following month, "Mandy" was featured in Nickolodeon's TV movie *Zoey 101*: *Spring Break-Up*, as well as on the show's soundtrack album. A cover version of "Yo Ho (A Pirate's Life For Me)" from *Pirates of the Caribbean* became part of the *Disneymania 4* compilation album, which was released on April 4. That summer the guys went on tour as an opening act for Aly & AJ in support of their yet-to-be-released album, and they recorded the theme song for season two of the Disney Channel series *American Dragon: Jake Long*.

With all that build-up, there was still no album for the JoBros' fans to buy. Phil McIntyre, manager of the group along with their father, explained, "Over the course of our time with Sony [which owns Columbia], we probably had 10 release dates, none of which was reached."

It certainly was about time on August 8, 2006, when *It's About Time* finally reached stores in what turned out to be only a limited release by Columbia (meaning about 50,000 copies reached the marketplace). It barely made a ripple. Considering all of the work that the Jonas Brothers had been doing to promote their music, this must have been an emotionally debilitating blow.

"It was disappointing," admitted McIntyre. "We'd never gone to Top 40, and Sony never put together a proper radio plan. Steve Greenberg did an amazing job of imagining a fan base at a grassroots level, but we were missing that key exposure."

Making the situation even worse was the fact that due to management changes at Columbia, somehow Kevin, Joe and Nick got lost in the shuffle. The new powers at the label simply didn't know what to do with the group and they weren't overly impressed with how the music had been doing up until that point.

"Along the way there were definitely times when we thought, 'Oh, great, not again!'" Joe stated. "Like when we'd go up on the charts and then we'd disappear. We'd be so frustrated and wonder when the big break was going to happen. But patience really pays off. We just continued practicing and waiting and writing songs."

For the rest of 2006 there was definitely some progress, most notably with Nick's solo song "Joy to the World (A Christmas Prayer)" on *Joy to the World: The Ultimate Christmas Collection* in October, and in that same month their cover version of "Poor Unfortunate Souls" was part of the soundtrack for *The Little Mermaid*. A bit of traction was made with "Year 3000," the second single from *It's About Time*, which gained a decent amount of airplay on Radio Disney. But it was too little too late as far as

Columbia was concerned, and as 2006 turned into 2007, the Jonases were set free of their contract. For Nick, Joe and Kevin, it was definitely something of a mutual decision. The boys felt that they weren't being given the label support they deserved, particularly after all their hard work in 2005 and 2006. Columbia, for its part, showed little interest in putting the needed push behind the guys.

The search began for a new label that they could call home.

Chapter 11

At Home in the Mouse House

It's become pretty obvious to anyone paying attention that the Walt Disney Company is now the premier driving force behind some of the biggest tween and teen phenomena in the world via its combination of the Disney Channel and its music label, Hollywood Records.

When it was first introduced to the public in 1983, the Disney Channel was a cable network desperately in search of an identity. Its programming consisted largely of material geared to the very young (actors dressed as Disney characters in shows like *Welcome to Pooh Corner* and *Dumbo's Circus*) and broadcasts of classic Disney animated shorts.

Over the years original programming such as *Kids Incorporated* (about a group of kids who form a pop group), *Good Morning, Miss Bliss* (a sitcom starring original *Parent Trap* star Hayley Mills) and *The New Mickey Mouse Club* (which introduced the world to Britney Spears, Justin Timberlake and Christina Aguilera) debuted and did okay in the ratings but hardly set the world on fire.

It wasn't until the years 2000 to 2003 that the Disney Channel truly began to

The Suite Life and *High School Musical*'s Ashley Tisdale with the Jonas Brothers.

connect with audiences, with *Even Stevens*, *Kim Possible* and *Lizzie McGuire* achieving new ratings highs for the network. Lizzie McGuire a.k.a. Hilary Duff became Disney's first tween sensation, and for the first time in quite a while, the Mouse House took a popular actress from its stable and molded her into a pop singer.

From that point on, success built on success, with *That's So Raven* (starring Raven-Symoné, who would go on to star in the highly successful *Cheetah Girls* movies) and *The Suite Life of Zack and Cody*, which starred twins Dylan and Cole Sprouse, Ashley Tisdale and Brenda Song.

In 2006, things *really* exploded with the smash success of the original Disney Channel TV movie *High School Musical*, making instant stars of Zac Efron, Vanessa Hudgens, Corbin Bleu and others, followed by the debut of actress/singer Miley Cyrus, whose unprecedented hit *Hannah Montana* turned her into a superstar.

And then there's Hollywood Records, which was founded in 1989 but has truly come into its own in recent years by tapping into the appeal of acting and singing double-threats — Hilary Duff, Jesse McCartney, Aly & AJ, *Heroes'* star Hayden Panettiere, The Cheetah Girls, Corbin Bleu, Miley Cyrus, Vanessa Hudgens and Demi Lovato.

Disney is the company with the Midas touch, armed with the uncanny ability to zero in on talent that will appeal to tweens

and teens in a major way. It's within that environment that the Jonas Brothers found themselves less than a month after leaving Columbia Records.

Everything changed for Kevin, Nick and Joe on February 8, 2007, when Disney announced that the band had been signed to Hollywood Records, with Bob Cavallo, chairman of Disney's Buena Vista Music Group, enthusing: "We are delighted to have the Jonas Brothers at Hollywood Records. They are talented and focused on making a great album. Their energy is infectious, and potential limitless."

Issuing a statement, the Jonases responded in kind: "We are fortunate to have this incredible opportunity to deliver noteworthy music to our fans. To continue building our careers in this industry with Hollywood Records is one step closer in achieving our dreams."

Believe it or not, that wasn't all the good news the guys received that day! Topps Confections announced a multi-million dollar deal with the brothers Jonas to serve as spokesmen for Baby Bottle Pop candy. Offered Topps' Art Weinstock, "We are thrilled to partner with the Jonas Brothers. . . . The Jonas Brothers' re-imagining of the Baby Bottle Pop theme song will have kids rocking out at one of their favorite theme songs sung by one of today's hottest groups."

According to Kevin, Nick and Joe, almost from the moment their signatures were signed to the Disney contract it seemed as though their fortunes had turned

around. Mused Nick, "We realized that right after our video started playing on the Disney Channel, a lot of people started showing up at the shows. It was just a different thing. It was a pretty cool moment. We suddenly had an average of 2,000 people at our shows, whereas before that we were lucky if it was 200."

"I think Disney had a *major* part in this," Joe said. "Before the Disney push, we were seeing a slight change, but right away, after they put the first video on Disney Channel, on our MySpace page we suddenly had hundreds of thousands of friend

> **Kevin, Joe and Nick are the real deal — incredible musicians, phenomenal performers, charismatic stars.**

requests in an hour. It was just unbelievable to see how crazy the response was. Our fan base grew faster than ever. We had so many more fans in the course of one month than we did in two years. Disney is just knocking balls out of the park right now with amazing things, and we're so glad to be a part of it. When we signed with Hollywood Records, we knew that the Disney Channel would play our videos, and we immediately got so excited. We are so blessed."

Noted Nick: "Disney is the best thing that has happened to our career so far, and we believe that it can lead to all sorts of things. It was important to us that the label guys get the band — which the people at Hollywood did." Joe added, "They must have been familiar with us beforehand,

because they'd seen us at shows when we had opened for Jesse McCartney."

Hollywood Records general manager Abbey Konowitch pointed out, "We've been incredibly successful in the teen-pop field, but we've been looking for a boy band. And here was one that was already developed." Disney's Gary Marsh added, "Kevin, Joe and Nick are the real deal — incredible musicians, phenomenal performers, charismatic stars. An act like the Jonas Brothers doesn't come along very often. This is a giant coup for the Disney Channel."

It wasn't *all* about business where the guys were concerned; one of the first things they did after being signed was to play a concert at their old school, Eastern Christian High School, in North Haledon, New Jersey. This, according to Kevin Sr., was a way of saying thank you to the school for being so understanding when the boys had to miss classes due to auditions and the like. Said Kevin Sr.: "They always understood about the boys' schedule. The school treated us really well and we want to give something back." After giving back to their community, the boys and the label got straight to work to build the Jonas Brothers into international superstars in one short year.

Chapter 12

Stars of the Future

Disney was well aware of what it had with the Jonas Brothers, and a plan quickly came together to build such a high profile for the group that by the time their debut disc on Hollywood Records was released in August 2007, there would be an entire fan base dying to get their hands on it.

In March 2007 the boys became a part of Disney history when they contributed "Kids of the Future" to the soundtrack of *Meet the Robinsons*, a song that was an updated version of the Kim Wilde song "Kids of America."

Said an excited Joe, "It definitely makes us happy that one day you'll be able to go through the Disney library and find that song there." Kevin added, "We loved doing the song and felt that the video for it looked awesome and it made people really connect with us."

On a more personal front, the guys agreed to headline the Carnival For a Cure, an event held on March 11 at New York's Metropolitan Pavilion, devoted to raising money to help find a cure for diabetes. As gathered fans quickly discovered, there was a personal reason for their involvement.

When the guys took to the stage, Nick stepped up to the microphone and asked the audience who among them had diabetes. A number of hands went up, among them Nick's! "I was diagnosed while we were on tour in November 2005," Nick explained. "I had all the classic symptoms — I was thirsty all the time, I lost a lot of weight and I was acting moody. My doctor told me that my blood sugar was 700, which meant that I had diabetes.

"I had an emotional breakdown," he continued earnestly, "since I really had no

idea what diabetes was all about. I wondered, 'Why me?' Then I asked myself, 'Why not me?' and realized that I might be able to help other kids with diabetes."

Nick went on to detail the fact that he had to take insulin injections several times a day, but that the process was made easier by using the OmniPod System, a wireless, continuous insulin delivery system that would eliminate the need for injections. As Carolyn Gershenson, a diabetes educator, explained: "The important thing for Nick was that he be able to manage his insulin in a way that complemented his lifestyle. The OmniPod System made it possible for him to use the best therapy for insulin-requiring diabetes — continuous insulin therapy — in a very discreet, easy and unencumbered way, and without interfering with his activities as a teenager and performer. The pod that adheres to the body is small, discreet and tube-free."

Instead of coming across as depressed to the crowd, Nick definitely had an optimistic outlook about the situation. "At first I was worried that diabetes would keep me from performing and recording and doing everything a teenager likes to do," he said. "I want to let kids know that it doesn't have to be so hard. The most important thing is to never,

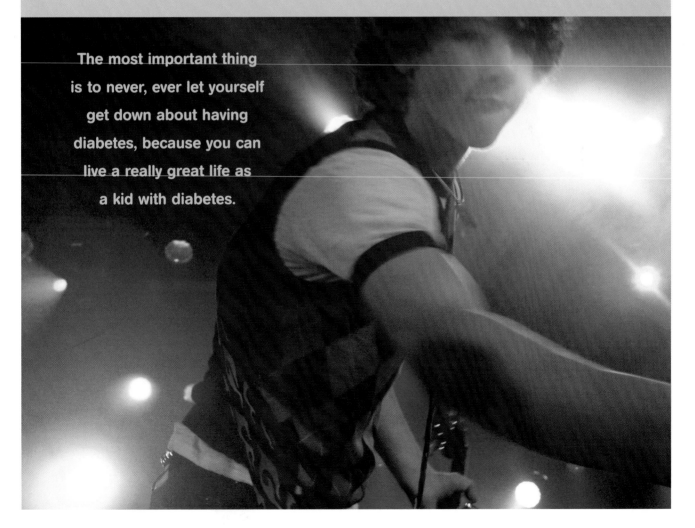

The most important thing
is to never, ever let yourself
get down about having
diabetes, because you can
live a really great life as
a kid with diabetes.

ever let yourself get down about having diabetes, because you can live a really great life as a kid with diabetes."

The way that Nick shared his condition so honestly with the public was something that many people admired, among them chairman-elect of the Diabetes Research Institute Foundation, Tom Stern. "We are incredibly inspired by the courage that Nick demonstrated by announcing that he is dealing with the daily challenge of type 1 diabetes," he said. "We are grateful to the entire Jonas family for sharing this very personal message and for supporting the efforts of the Diabetes Research Institute."

Concluded Nick on the subject: "I just want kids my age and all kinds of kids to feel comfortable talking about it, because I've heard stories of people nervous to tell anyone. With something like this, you always have to take your time before you go public with it. It took us until we — me, especially — learned how to take care of it. Once we felt like we had an approach where we could manage, we just felt it was time to let people know. Since then, I've gotten so many emails and letters from kids with their stories. They all have their own individual stories, and the fact that I was able to share mine and hear theirs was very cool."

Diabetes is a chronic disease that affects 23.6 million Americans — about 8% of the population. The number of people with diabetes is on the rise, up 13.5% between 2005 and

their bloodstreams, leading to two main types of diabetes. Type 1 (which Nick has) occurs when the pancreas can't produce insulin. People with type 1 diabetes have to inject insulin into their bodies to prevent too much glucose from building up in their bloodstreams. Some people with type 1 diabetes give themselves regular injections, and others, like Nick, use automatic insulin pumps to correct their blood sugar. Type 1 diabetes is also known as "juvenile diabetes," because it mostly affects people under 30. In type 2 diabetes, the pancreas doesn't make enough insulin, or the body can't use the insulin it makes. Some people can keep their type 2 diabetes under control with a proper diet and exercise, while others also need medication and insulin.

Diabetes affects people's energy levels, so diabetics have to pay careful attention to how they're feeling and check their blood sugar levels throughout the day. Type 1 diabetics who rely on insulin injections have to calculate their doses carefully, adjusting for meals and exercise. Diabetics also have to pay special attention to what they eat, so they can keep their glucose levels as close to normal as possible. People with diabetes have a higher risk of complications like depression, digestive problems, dental problems, heart disease and vision loss, but if they follow the health care plans made for them carefully, they can lead ordinary lives, or in Nick Jonas's case — extraordinary ones.

2007, but it is properly diagnosed more often than in the past. Diabetes has been called "the epidemic of the twenty-first century" by the International Diabetes Federation, which estimates about 380 million people will have diabetes worldwide by 2025 if major preventative measures are not taken. Aside from Nick Jonas, many other famous musicians have (or had) diabetes including Johnny Cash, Miles Davis, Tommy Lee, BB King, Patti LaBelle, Meat Loaf, Syd Barrett, James Brown, Neil Young and David Crosby.

During digestion, the body breaks down food into smaller components like glucose (or sugar). A healthy body regulates glucose levels with insulin, a hormone produced in the pancreas. People with diabetes can't naturally regulate the amount of glucose in

The Disney connection for the Jonas Brothers continued in April 2007 when the guys were featured on *Disneymania 5*, performing "I Wanna Be Like You" from the 1967 animated film *The Jungle Book*. Other artists on the disc included Miley Cyrus, Corbin Bleu and The Cheetah Girls.

Hollywood Records lined up the guys as an opening act for Jesse McCartney's April 13 Boca Raton concert. For the trio it was a bit like history repeating itself as they had opened for McCartney back in 2005, but this time there was something very different about the evening: this time, the Jonas Brothers were the bigger stars. Commented musiqtone.com, "One might not have realized that there was a Jesse McCartney concert. The only reminder to those realizing that the Jonas Brothers stole the show was a giant Jesse McCartney banner behind them."

Continuing to push the band — but in a good way — Disney had them shoot the video for their song "Hold On," and perform at a Wal-Mart in California. As spring turned into summer and the release date of their second album approached, the Jonas Brothers were everywhere — performing and promoting. And the new record wasn't the only project in the works.

In May, the Disney Channel announced that the green light had been given for a new TV pilot called *J.O.N.A.S.*, standing for Junior Operatives Networking As Spies and originally saw Kevin, Joe and Nick as a trio of rock performers who also happen to be spies out to save the world from bad guys who want to take it over. The entertainment trade magazines described the pilot as a cross between *The Monkees*, *Get Smart* and the *Austin Powers* feature films.

With the arrival of July came word from Disney that Kevin, Nick and Joe would be appearing in an episode of *Hannah Montana* alongside Miley Cyrus, and would be starring in an original Disney Channel TV movie *Camp Rock*, described by the network as being about "a teen girl who desperately wants to spend her summer at a prestigious rock camp, but can attend only if she works in the kitchen as one of the cooks," and she is "discovered" by Joe Jonas's character.

Hollywood Records held a *major* media event in the middle of July at New York's Samsung Experience, where they heralded a new form of technology called the CDVU+, which the Jonas Brothers would debut with their sophomore album. Combining the best of "what physical product and the Internet have to offer," the CDVU+ allows fans to be "fanatics" with: an easy-to-navigate digital magazine format; a 50-page interactive digital package that is printable and can be downloaded and then accessed both on and offline; song lyrics; 10 different video segments with the band; behind the scenes footage; video guitar instruction sessions with the band; a letter from the Jonas Brothers; 75 printable photos of the guys; a link to Flickr.com and JonasBrothers.com offering fans continually updated information and content, including new photo albums and videos of the Jonases on tour; a customizable autographed poster creator where fans can upload their own image into different band scenarios; and special hidden links to exclusive content only available via CDVU+. Another major selling point: the product is eco-friendly, made out of 100% recyclable material.

With the release of their self-titled album mere weeks away, the guys embarked on a North American tour that launched on June 25 in their home state of New Jersey and continued until October 21 at the South Carolina State Fair, with 44 dates in between. What was really cool about this particular tour was that the guys decided to give it a unique theme. Considering that they had been home-schooled for so long, they had missed out on some of the things that most kids experienced, like prom. So they asked fans to come to the shows dressed appropriately for a prom and decorated the venues with prom paraphernalia.

Partway through the tour, Joe observed: "It becomes a really cool, big party when you get into the venue with everyone else. Girls have actually even been dressing up in prom dresses and corsages, like full on. It's really awesome. And, for all the guys out there, it's a great place to be."

Chapter 13
Jonas Brothers
ON THE RECORD

There is something about the Disney world that has become synonymous with the word "magic," and that would undoubtedly be a word that comes to the mind of the Jonas Brothers when asked about their experience with the Mouse House.

When the trio was signed to Hollywood Records, they came in the door with a definite game plan. Columbia had had them either collaborate on songs with others or take tracks whole-cloth from different writers; the Jonas Brothers were determined that their follow-up disc would represent them completely. *They* would be playing the instruments and writing the songs.

As Kevin explained it: "When we signed to Hollywood, we told the label, 'Hey, we have some demos of songs we've been writing for the past year and a half.' We thought it'd be so funny to just record those songs for the album to see what we could get away with. But those turned out to be the record. What was really amazing is that the first record took us, like, a year-and-a-half to make. The second one took 21 days, including weekends. It was one of the best experiences. We were there recording and were involved from the first beat of the drums and the first time something was put on tape, right through to the end. From start to finish, it was an awesome experience."

One of their saving graces was being teamed up with producer John Fields, who had previously worked with such artists as Lifehouse, Switchfoot and Rooney. It was reportedly a request from the Jonases themselves, who were fans of what Fields had done with Switchfoot's album *The Beautiful Letdown*, which, incidentally, was the producer's first big hit, having sold 2.5 million copies. For his part, Fields agreed to produce the album following a meeting with the guys in which they played their original songs on acoustic guitars. They immediately began working on *Jonas Brothers*, which Fields described as "one of the most fun times I've ever had in the studio; everything was so positive and there was zero stress."

Noted Kevin: "The album was very much a collaborative process. It's definitely our baby, but John completely understood our vision and made sure we were there to help him guide the process every day of recording. We rented out a house in Studio City that we called 'Rock House,' living there for the whole month of February [2007] and working from 11 a.m. to 11 p.m. in the attached facility called Underbelly Studios. It was a really awesome, one-of-a-kind experience."

Praised Joe in a *Mix* profile of Fields: "From the beginning, we connected with him. Since the first song we did together, he

has always been open to our ideas, almost as if we were co-producing."

"We're very hands-on as a group," Kevin related. "We write and build our songs, and when someone once asked John how he does this, he said, 'I just listen to the boys,' which was such an honor for us. Sometimes you meet somebody and it just works perfectly right away. The connection was there for all of us from the start."

Added Nick: "John loves music and is very open-minded. He's very fast, which helps us because we work fast, too. During the recording of our album, we really became close. John is like another Jonas

John Taylor and Nick chat between takes on the set of "S.O.S."

Brother, and I think that's why we got such good results with him."

It also didn't hurt that they had personally gone through a lot, which helped them evolve between discs. "When we signed with Hollywood Records, at that point we really knew who we were as the Jonas Brothers," shared Nick. "We kind of took a hold of that and started writing some really cool songs while we were on the road. I think the lyrics on our second album were filled with a lot more personal experiences

and things like that. For that reason, I think that people can really connect with it, and that's cool."

Jonas Brothers kicked off with the hit single "S.O.S.," which Nick explained was the result of him trying to sort his way through some difficult personal experiences by turning them into a song. "It was really cool that I was able to write the song, come back from what happened and it was finished very quickly," he said. "I always write better songs when I have a strong inspiration for them,

Joe, Nick and Kevin on the set of the video for "Hold On."

and for this song I really had a strong inspiration." Considering its origins, it's a little surprising that the track is as rocking as it is. Joe explained: "We love dance music and we were glad we could put it into a song. It's a song about kind of being dissed by a girl and it hurts more than she knows. Sounds heavy, but it's upbeat." This is actually Kevin's favorite track on the album. "Nicholas wrote this one by himself," he said. "He had gone through a bad night and had a hard time,

and he ended up putting it into this song. It's very dancey, has a fun beat to it and it's a good time." The video for "S.O.S." was filmed in June 2007 on the historic (and reportedly haunted) *Queen Mary* in Long Beach, California. Featuring a cameo from *Hannah Montana*'s Moises Arias (Rico), the story in the video mirrored the lyrics of the song with the boys running into girl troubles aboard the ship.

"Hold On" was actually the first single

from the album, which, according to Kevin, "really captured the transition from the first album to this one. First there was 'Kids of the Future' — that was the really evolutionary song — but this was our song that we wrote, and people heard what we wanted to say." It's Joe's feeling that the song is about "holding on because you don't want to give up on love," while Nick believes it's "a good arena rock song that people go crazy for when they hear it." The same director who worked on "S.O.S.," Declan Whitebloom, also helmed the video for "Hold On." The boys are rocking out in a house when a powerful windstorm blows in, knocking down everything including the walls, but the JoBros manage to hold on.

"Good Night and Goodbye" is looked upon by the guys as the perfect break-up song. Offered Kevin: "Nick said it best when he said that when he wants to break up with a girl, he just wants to say, 'Peace, I'm out of here.' So the song captures that moment when you're done with a crazy relationship." Nick concurred, adding, "It's something that everybody goes through — when they're going through a break-up and you're just saying goodbye and getting ready to move on." Joe believed this was "the most musical song we have on the album with a lot going on. We wrote it so fast and had a great time. It was a crazy experience in the studio writing it, because there was a lot of drumming and guitar playing."

For Nick, "That's Just the Way We Roll" is "a cool song about hanging out with your friends and having a good time. It's pretty much the theme song to our life. I think everybody has some times when they need to lose it a little, and that's what this one's about." In addition, Kevin felt that it was an opportunity to go a bit zany calling it a "very fun, outgoing and weird song with strange lyrics. I mean, 'There's a whale in the pool with my mother'? We were like, 'What is that?'" What it was, said Joe, was an opportunity for them to "just go crazy."

"Hello Beautiful," according to Nick, was a song written while the guys were on the road which comes "from personal experience." Kevin said that when they wrote it, they knew that it would "stay acoustic. It just needs to be that way, and the girls really seem to like it." Joe elaborated, "We wrote it on tour and it's about missing a girl while you're on tour and all you want is to get on a plane and fly to her."

Kevin calls "Still in Love With You" an amazing song, which almost began to write itself while they were in the midst of a different track. "We found our niche," he said, "and really went to another place with this song. We wanted to talk about how this girl left and she wants to be gone from your life, but you're still in love with her, you can't get over her and you want her back really bad. We've all felt that way before and we wanted to write a song about it." Added Joe, "This is about a break-up, but you still have feelings for that person. Even when they might have moved on, you're still stuck in that situation remembering when everything was fun."

Nick referred to this one as "one of my favorite songs that we've recorded."

"Australia" was written out of a desire, according to Kevin, to come up with something "obscure and funny, and this song really found its way into our hearts and we really love it. We all love accents and we always wanted to go to Australia, so it's a funny song and the beat is amazing. It has a ripping guitar solo." Speaking of accents, Joe pointed out, "We love Australian accents — especially me — and if a girl has an accent, doesn't matter which kind, I'm probably in love with her." Kevin reflected that "originally our dad said, 'You're going to have to rewrite that to make it more neutral,' but our A&R guy was more like, 'I love that whole Australia thing, I want to keep that,' which was fine with us, because we thought it was pretty awesome."

Joe enjoyed "Games" because it was "a really fun song to record with a lot of reggae feel put into it," which, according to Nick, "was really inspired by the band The Police. We wanted to make that song a little different from the rest of the record. We were listening to a few Police songs and we said, 'Let's do it like that.' So we recorded it and added that whole reggae vibe to it." As Kevin remembered, the track was written on their first tour with Jesse McCartney back in 2005. "We wrote it with our band," he said, "and it's a really awesome song. We had a really good time doing it."

"When You Look Me in the Eyes," originally written for Nick's solo album, was "reworked it so that it would better fit with our sound," reflected Nick. Added Joe, "It's a song about what happens when a girl looks you in the eyes and you just know that everything is going to be okay. It's an amazing feeling." The song was rearranged while they were working with producer John Fields, who's known "for big, rocked-out power ballads, and it worked out so well that we knew we had to have it on the album no matter what," recalled Kevin. The video for this track spoke to that tradition of power ballads with acclaimed director Robert Hales delivering a black-and-white classic, which harkened back to videos for "Home Sweet Home" (Mötley Crüe), "Wanted Dead or Alive" (Bon Jovi) and "Every Rose Has its Thorn" (Poison). Providing fans with a glimpse of life on the road from the perspective of the Jonas Brothers, the video had over a million hits on YouTube after only one week.

As far as Joe is concerned, "Inseparable" is one of the most rocking songs on *Jonas Brothers*, and it's about "being thousands of miles away from that person, whoever it may be, and there's nothing that can break them — it's the love-conquers-distance kind of thing." Kevin added to that point by stating, "It says that even though I'm far away from you, you should know I really care about you and I want you to be here with me." Pointed out Nick, "I think that everybody once in a while has those long-distance relationships, and that's really what this song is about: promising to do anything to work it all out."

Kevin noted that "Just Friends" was

written about "growing up, knowing that you're in love with someone, but also realizing that you'll never be in a relationship, but then one day it happens and you know it was meant to be." Joe elaborated by saying, "You're carrying a secret love for a friend and you act like everything's cool, even though it isn't." Nick adds: "It's about a group of friends where there's a guy and a girl who are just good friends, but one of them is actually madly in love with the friend but can never admit it, because it would be awkward. But they always dream

of having that life in the future where they're together and in love. I think people connect with it, because everybody has had that kind of person in their lives."

The song "Hollywood" was inspired by the JoBros being signed to their new label and, said Joe, the "transition from Columbia Records over to Hollywood Records." Nick said, "We finally found somewhere we belong at Hollywood Records, which is a pretty cool thing." Kevin added, "It was a new label and the beginning of a new chapter in the Jonas Brothers' life."

The album wrapped up with "Kids of the Future," from the *Meet the Robinsons* soundtrack. Of its origin, Nick detailed: "A song that was first done by Kim Wilde as 'Kids of America.' We remade it for *Meet the Robinsons* and reworked it to 'Kids of the Future' to more fit in with the movie, and it was just this really cool, fun song. We opened our show with it and people really love it." Kevin believed this was "definitely a huge step for us. We loved it and felt that the video for the song looked awesome and it made people really connect with us." Another Declan Whitebloom–directed video, "Kids of the Future" showcased the Jonas Brothers performing in dark club setting mixed in with clips from *Meet the Robinsons*.

And *Jonas Brothers* really connected with the public from the moment it was released on August 7, 2007. It made its debut on the *Billboard* 200 chart at #5, with first week sales of 69,000 copies. "It's the happiest feeling ever when you see that you've reached #5," said a justifiably proud Joe. It dropped a bit from there, moving 41,000 copies in week two (moving down to #8) and in week three it dropped to #11 with sales of 35,000 copies. While this may sound as though it was a pretty serious drop off, it continued to sell consistently and, by February 20, 2008, was certified platinum (meaning sales of over 1,000,000 copies) by the RIAA.

All three Jonas brothers were pleased with the way their second album turned out, and by the evolution in their sound between their first and second discs. "Our music has evolved because we've all grown up quite a bit from the last record," Nick said. "We have all had so many maturing experiences over the last couple of years. It's been amazing. The lyrics and music are a little more advanced than the last one in the sense that we learned how to play our instruments a little better. As a result, we were able to come up with cooler chords."

"And this is different," elaborated Joe, "because it has a lot more electric guitar and a lot more loud music." Kevin explained: "I think our first album was a little more raw. Now our album is more tight. I think we figured out who we want to be and what we want to sound like. Plus our writing abilities had grown."

Their sound, as evidenced by both their albums and their live performances, was edgier than that of the vast majority of Disney-related performers. "We're definitely more of a rock band compared to a pop band," offered Joe. "We play our own instruments and write our own songs and go up on stage and play with our hearts. When people come to our concerts, I can definitely promise them that they'll have a good time, because the energy in the room is so much fun and the audience screams its heart out."

Chapter 14

The Best of Both Worlds

> **The whole thing is so amazing and cool, and our fans are the loudest fans you'll ever hear.**

It was exciting enough for the audience at the 2007 Teen Choice Awards when the Jonas Brothers took to the stage with Miley Cyrus to present an award. But at the podium they announced that they would be touring together in the near future — much to the delight of screaming fans.

That response was not exactly surprising, considering the ratings success the Disney Channel had on the night of August 17, when the trio guest starred in the "Me and Mr. Jonas and Mr. Jonas and Mr. Jonas" episode of *Hannah Montana*, which aired immediately after *High School Musical 2* and took in a *major* audience.

In the episode, Miley Stewart gets jealous when the Jonas Brothers show up, start hanging out with her father, Robbie Stewart, and begin writing songs with him, leaving Hannah Montana out of the mix. As Joe detailed: "In the episode, we're pretty much best friends with Billy Ray rather than Hannah. All he wants to do is hang out with us and Hannah gets upset. It was just a

really funny episode with a lot of great things in it." At the end of the episode, Hannah and the Jonas Brothers perform "We Got the Party (With Us)" together.

"It was amazing," Nick said with a big smile. "That was our first sitcom experience and it was really fun. For us it was a whole new animal and so different from concerts. It was pure fun getting in front of the camera and doing the lines. By the time it came to film, we had memorized our lines and weren't worried about that anymore. What we needed to focus on was the *delivery* of those lines."

Kevin pointed out: "We really found it to be so much fun and exciting and energetic. It was just us performing. We were in our element and everything felt right."

One of the things that they had *not* expected from the experience was how different it was to perform in front of a studio audience than it was to perform before a concert crowd, and, in the case of Nick and Joe, from a Broadway audience.

As Joe explained it, if you're in a concert and you mess up a lyric or on the guitar, there's no one yelling, "Cut, let's do it again."

"Plus," he said, "you don't practice for a week before a concert. You have a sound check and that's a little practice for you every night. *Hannah Montana* was just a completely different look on things, especially having never been on a television show with a live audience. One way it was similar to a concert is that so much is done beforehand and after for an hour-and-a-half concert, and the same is true for this 30-minute show. That 30 minutes is a week's worth of rehearsing, designing sets, cutting out scenes and more. Every day we had a new script, because they would either rewrite something, work something into the script or have an almost all-new script."

Observed Kevin: "*Hannah Montana* is filmed with a live audience, but our *J.O.N.A.S.* pilot was shot single camera and there was no live audience. That was different, because there was no one there to laugh or cheer. We liked doing both. And Miley is a great friend of ours, and it was great being with her."

Back in June, the guys performed with their pal Miley at Six Flags Magic Mountain in Valencia, California. Miley and the JoBros enjoyed the park together prior to their performances, and this may very well have been the place that the rumors began that Nick and Miley were dating. It eventually grew into a fairly big story and gained a lot of heat in the weeks and months to come. Both Nick and Miley claimed that while they were best friends and Miley and the Jonases loved hanging out with each other, there was never anything romantic between Nick and Miley.

Miley explained to the press, "Me and Nick Jonas were always being put together, but, no, we're just friends. . . . We're buddies. We hung out on tour and we're really close friends who love being together. We're very alike just because of what we do, but our

personalities are very different. He's very quiet and conservative, but I'm very opinionated, loud and crazy. Hanging out together is weird, because I'm like a tomboy who is very carefree and they're all a little bit more conservative and very put together, which is the opposite of how I am." It wasn't until the September 2008 issue of *Seventeen* magazine that the rumors were officially confirmed as true: Miley confessed that she and Nick did date but they had broken up at the end of 2007.

But back in October 2007 before any hearts were broken and the Best of Both Worlds tour was just kicking off, Miley Cyrus had proven herself to be one of the

biggest entertainment phenomena in decades. Her Disney Channel series *Hannah Montana* was garnering unprecedented ratings for the network, her CDs were selling unbelievable numbers and her tour — tickets for which went on sale on August 18 — was a sell-out in every city, usually within minutes of tickets going on sale. The tour, which was choreographed by *High School Musical*'s Kenny Ortega, was the hottest concert of 2007.

The Jonas Brothers were announced as the opening act for the tour, thus guaranteeing that the band, which was already skyrocketing in popularity, would be greeted by larger audiences than ever before. The tour was in support of Miley's double disc, *Hannah Montana 2: Meet Miley Cyrus*, but it seemed as though Kevin, Joe and Nick got an almost equal amount of attention from it.

"It's unbelievable," laughed Kevin in

regard to the response. "At some point you just have to ask yourself, 'What is going on?' We love what we do, we have an amazing time doing it and I couldn't ask for anything more. And the response from the fans — they're screaming, jumping up and down, singing all the words to every song. We have such a good time and the fans love to be so into it; they're so much fun every night. And for us, we go out there and try to play the best show that we can, giving our all no matter how many people are there. We're going to perform like there's 10,000 even if there are only 200 people. With us, we're so excited, because we're finally playing new songs with our new record and then we'll play an old song and people freak out."

Added Joe: "The whole thing is so amazing and cool, and our fans are the loudest fans you'll ever hear. We have such a fun time with our fans when we're on stage. It's such a blessing that they love our music, and watching them sing along with the songs, even the new ones, is really incredible."

Not surprisingly, their experience on the Best of Both Worlds tour reached a whole new level of excitement. "That show, playing the arenas, was a dream come true," said Kevin. "As a band, we really had a goal to elevate our performance musically, and introduce different types of music into our performance that will go into another song. So you might hear something and not recognize it right away, but then all of a sudden you realize that it's a song that we've been playing for five years now. We did 56 shows on that tour. Before that, we had played every little rock 'n' roll club in America on multiple tours. It's been an amazing journey the last couple of years."

Added Nick, "It was a really great time. You know, Miley and all of her people are just really fun and awesome to be around." "Every time we play, we learn so much and grow both as artists and a band," Joe pointed out.

Apparently Miley Cyrus learned a lot too, as she revealed in an interview with *Girls' Life* when asked about Jonas secrets. "I have one," she laughed, "about Kevin. Seriously, he acts like he doesn't care about style, that he just throws on something, but he is so obsessed with fashion. You don't even know. When we go hang out or even just go get ice cream, he's decked. He's got on the nicest jeans with the nicest shoes. He always looks awesome. You know, he actually told us he takes an hour-and-a-half to straighten his hair every morning. I told him why not just get that Japanese treatment, where it would just stay straight all the time. But he likes it to be curly when he gets out of the pool."

For fans who couldn't get or afford the sometimes ridiculous ticket mark-ups, Disney came up with the idea of releasing a 3D version of the concert to movie theaters. What initially seemed like just a gimmick ended up being anything but, when its opening weekend on just over 600 screens pulled in a record-breaking $31 million and ended up with a domestic gross of over $60 million — this on a $7 million investment on Disney's part.

The Jonas Brothers stayed with the Best of Both Worlds tour from October 18 through January 9, 2008. At that point, the tour was extended to March 9, but the Jonas Brothers had to step down. They were about to embark on the next phase of their career: headlining their *own* major tour.

Chapter 15

Look Me in the Eyes

The Jonas Brothers wrapped up 2007, a banner and busy year for them, by performing live, with Miley Cyrus, on *Dick Clark's New Year's Rocking Eve*. Co-host Ryan Seacrest announced that night that the Jonas Brothers would be launching their Look Me in the Eyes tour beginning on January 31.

Shortly before the Jonas Brothers wrapped their stint on the Best of Both Worlds tour, they had struck a deal with the country's largest live music company, Live Nation, to headline their own tour.

"Known for its global tours with such pop culture icons as Madonna, the Rolling Stones and The Police, to name a few, Live Nation has inked a long term worldwide touring deal with the platinum selling music phenomenon, Jonas Brothers," proclaimed an official announcement. "The deal, the first of its kind for an emerging act, is expected to play more than 140 theaters and arenas around the world . . . The announcement comes on the heels of a wildly successful year for Jonas Brothers, which included their platinum album and

their special guest appearance on the sold out Best of Both Worlds arena tour, massive Internet and Top 40 radio exposure, and countless TV appearances and magazine covers. *Billboard* magazine also named the group the pop tour break out pick for 2008."

Live Nation's Bruce Kapp said: "The band creates pandemonium wherever they go. They sell out dates instantly and always leave their loyal fans wanting more."

"The Jonas Brothers are without a doubt one of the most promising young touring bands working today," added Live Nation's Brad Wavra. "Over the next two years we will work alongside the band, management and their record label to grow

Jonas Brothers' fan base and establish them as one of the most successful touring bands in music."

Kevin, Nick and Joe enthused: "The level of commitment and passion that everyone at Live Nation has shown for our band has been inspiring. Together we are going to bring our show to millions of our fans around the world. We couldn't be more excited about our future together."

Some may have wondered whether the Bros had a large enough fan base to support an arena tour. Would such a tour be successful? The answer — a resounding yes — came almost immediately after tickets went on sale.

No matter how big or small a concert may be, Kevin, Nick and Joe play with all their heart. And they go through the same pre-show warm-up before appearing on stage to the thunderous applause and screams of their appreciative fans.

"We do a couple of things," Nick explained. "I start to focus for about two hours before the show and get my head into the game in terms of what we're about to do. I get changed, get ready, do my hair, do warm-ups and we kind of have a little bit of a bonding session before the show where we say, 'Have a great show, man; love you, guys; you're doing great, keep it up; let's rock this!' It's just a good family vibe all together."

Joe added, "We have a lockdown where no one will leave the room and no one will come in. We just become really focused. We have vocal warm-ups for about 10 minutes and from there we pray. I do stretches and push-ups and things like that. I get myself warmed up so that on stage I can move around a lot. It sounds funny, but you want your body warmed up and stretched out because you don't want to hurt anything on stage. For instance, you don't want to cramp your leg up if you're doing a crazy kick or jumping off something."

Following a show there's a bit of a ritual as well, as the guys come off the stage, the sound of the crowd fading in the distance. Joe related: "It's so cool. You feel like you've accomplished something great. We want to do it all over again, but in a good way. We're like, 'Man, that was great.' We just can't stop

The band creates pandemonium wherever they go.

smiling. We're in a pool of sweat, but we're still smiling."

"We always take a couple of minutes to cool off, relax and just chill for a couple of minutes," Nick added, "because you have so much energy pumping when you're on stage that when you get off, you need a minute to just relax. Then we have to psyche ourselves up again the next night."

In one interview, Joe was asked whether he preferred arenas or more intimate club settings, to which he responded: "We love arenas because they're arenas, which is really cool. But we also love playing small venues, because it gives us a chance to be more intimate with our fans and really see their beautiful faces."

Speaking of fans, the guys do admit that things can sometimes get a little hairy with the fans' determination just to say hello to them wherever they are.

"Most of the time, we put where we're going to be online and the fans just show up,"

said Kevin. "But even when we don't tell them, they somehow manage to figure it out anyway. It's weird how they're able to do that."

Laughed Joe: "Whenever we go to a new city on the tour, we usually drive overnight and we usually get to the hotel we're staying at at, like, three or four in the morning. But what's funny is that when we pull away from an arena at night, we'll see eight or nine cars driving behind us, just waiting for us to stop at a gas station or a McDonald's. Sometimes we'll have a seven-hour drive overnight, we're asleep in the bus and they'll be wide awake and driving, just to say hi or maybe hoping that we'll get a flat tire so they can offer to help fix it. Though I'm not sure a 14-year-old girl is going to be able to lift a bus and change a flat.

"A weirder experience," he added, "was that we were eating dinner in the Bahamas, and the manager came over and said that a lady was in the front who said she was our mother and wanted to surprise us by joining us for dinner. That would have been fun, except for the fact that our mother was already there with us, so that was a bit odd."

The Jonas Brothers' tour bus wasn't really hard for fans to spot on this particular tour. First of all, their name was painted on the side of it. Second, there was a wrap around the vehicle on which fans at every stop were encouraged to write down a message for Joe, Kevin and Nick.

Chapter 16

Team Jonas

There is no question that the Jonas Brothers has become a well-oiled machine, and not just in terms of the performances of Kevin, Nick and Joe. Behind the scenes, the guys seem to be in the best of hands thanks to a select group of people.

First off, their father, Kevin Jonas Sr., is ever-present, in on all of the decision-making that affects his kids. As a result, he works closely with the rest of the team in all manners Jonas.

Johnny Wright, of Wright Entertainment, a key part of the JoBros' team, is one of the most successful music managers ever. Born in Hyannis, Massachusetts, his career began when he was 19, as a DJ at a local roller-skating rink. He managed to capture the attention of radio station WCOD in Cape Cod, which hired him as a DJ. There he met with New Kids on the Block manager Maurice Starr, who recognized Johnny's talent and hired him to be the band's tour manager. He worked with the New Kids on major tours until the group decided to take a year off from their whirlwind superstar schedule.

After working as a manager for other bands, in 1993 he relocated to Orlando, Florida, where Wright began collaborating with Lou Pearlman and Transcon Entertainment. Two years later he was manager of the Backstreet Boys and, three years after that, he began working with *NSync. During his time with them he also signed on Britney Spears, who sold upwards of 60 million albums while they worked together.

Wright Entertainment Group eventually joined forces with Creative Management Group, forming Wright-Crear Management, which allowed Johnny to work with Janet Jackson, among others. In August 2006 he

Johnny Wright (far right) joins the Jonas Brothers and Kobe Bryant backstage at the 2008 MTV VMAs.

began working with the Jonas Brothers and has played an integral role in their success ever since.

Working in conjunction with Kevin Sr. and Johnny Wright is Philip McIntyre, who earned his stripes taking care of everything Britney Spears needed while on tour. Eventually he formed Philymack Entertainment, which is described as a full-service management company devoted to musicians and entertainment professionals. Phil is credited as a producer on the Jonas Brothers' 3D concert movie and is excited about the innovative ways they use technology to connect with their fans. "YouTube, MySpace, from day one have been an integral part as far as building fans and communicating with the Jonas Brothers fan base," he explained. "It's a natural fit, it's who they are, it's something they truly enjoy doing." In regards to the band itself, he added: "They write their own music, they play their own instruments. These guys are true artists. They leave it all on the stage. The fans react to it and they know how much the boys are putting into it. Therefore they feel like that journey's just as special to them as it is to the boys."

Another member of Team Jonas who used to be a key part of Team Britney is Felicia Culotta. She spent years as Britney's personal assistant (and close friend) and played the teacher in the video for "Baby One More Time." Felicia was brought into the Jonas Brothers' camp and has become an important part of it ever since. In a December 2007 interview with the New York *Daily News*, Felicia described working with the Jonas Brothers as "a totally positive experience. They are wonderful and I feel so lucky to be with such sweet people."

Rounding it all off is head of security Big Rob, who also served as Britney Spears' bodyguard. In her mom Lynne Spears' memoir, she described Rob as "a delightful man": "Funny, sweet, and congenial, that dear man became part of our family. We felt so safe with him around." In fact, Jamie Lynn Spears' signature character on *All That*,

Big Rob joins the JoBros to perform "Burnin' Up" on *Good Morning America*.

bodyguard Thelma Stump, was based in part on Big Rob! According to an interview he gave to jonasbrothersfan.com, he hasn't had to get "physical" with any fans just yet. No doubt they're intimidated by the sight of him — Rob is absolutely a giant of a man, but there's a certain teddy-bear quality to him as well. Big Rob keeps in touch with the JoBros fans by blogging on Ryan Seacrest's site from time to time, giving them updates on what he and the guys are up to. Of course, Rob debuted his rapping skills in the first single off *A Little Bit*

Longer, "Burnin' Up," and the boys call him their "major confidant."

Crucial to Team Jonas are the guys who fill out the sound of the Jonas Brothers, on stage and in the studio. The boys have called their backing band their "closest friends on the road" and it's obviously true from their dynamic on stage and backstage. John "J.T." Taylor is the band's musical director and a guitarist. He lives in California and makes his own solo music under the name "J.T." (check him out on MySpace). Also a Jersey boy like the brothers Jonas, Greg "Garbo"

John Taylor, Ryan Liestman and Greg Garbowsky with Nick, Joe and Kevin during the Burning Up tour.

Garbowsky plays bass for the Jonas Brothers and has been with the band since 2005. Greg has co-written two songs with the JoBros so far: "Games" from *Jonas Brothers* and "Tonight" from *A Little Bit Longer*. A relative newcomer to the band, Jack "Flawless" Lawless started playing drums (and percussion) for JB in early 2007, replacing former drummer Alexander Noyes. On the keyboards is Ryan Liestman. Ryan is the frontman of his own band, The Rule, and toured as the opening act for Cyndi Lauper in 2006.

And of course, when the Jonas Brothers go on tour, the regular team explodes into a small army — tour and production managers, roadies, additional security, drivers, costume stylists, lighting and staging technicians. . . . Kevin, Joe and Nick know how many people work so very hard to make their shows the best possible for the fans and appreciate it. Joe explained how close the road crew and the band become: "Our crew is like our family. Everybody's really cool and we get along with everybody." From the actual blood relations to the extended tour crew, the Jonas Brothers really are a family band.

Chapter 17

Don't Forget Camp Rock!

For the Disney Channel, the original concept for *Camp Rock* was to create a new franchise in the tradition of *High School Musical*: find a group of talented performers, add a mixture of song and dance, and stir. It was also an opportunity to give a starring role to actress Demi Lovato, who the Mouse House thought had the potential to become a genuine star.

But the project took on a whole new dimension when it became a vehicle for the Jonas Brothers and a test of whether or not Kevin, Joe and Nick would be able to crossover from the world of music to acting. After the experience, Kevin commented, "I never thought about it, but I really loved acting. Hopefully we have a long future with the Disney Channel."

As Joe explained, he liked the basic idea of starring in a Disney Channel film, and when the subject of *Camp Rock* was brought up, he was immediately interested. "I auditioned for it last summer [2007] and they told me I got it. The producers also told me that if Nick and Kevin wanted to be in it, some roles could be expanded for them."

Offered an excited Gary Marsh, Disney Channel's worldwide entertainment president, "Joe has that Mick Jagger image that he portrays on stage. It's who he is, he's a performer. He's a very natural performer. He'd never really acted before. I thought he did a fantastic job. And honestly, it's a pretty nuanced performance. It seemed like out of the three of the brothers he was the right guy for the role."

"As a band," Nick said, "we love to act as well as sing and I think acting will be a major part in our career as well. We hope to be the kind of artists that can sing, perform, go on tour and act as well. And we did do the *Hannah Montana* episode and our pilot, *J.O.N.A.S.*, both of which were really big training tools."

The film's subject matter — a summer sleep-away camp for aspiring performers and a romance that forms there — was appealing to the guys. Smiled Joe: "Summer romances are good. We all went to camp a

and I fell in. She never talked to me again. But that's okay. Maybe this movie will remind her of that."

Kevin was quick to point out, however, "We've never been to a camp like Camp Rock, but we wish we had." Nick also has fond real-life camp memories, "I did go to camp for two years in a row and it was definitely a place I looked forward to going to."

A rock and roll twist on the *Cinderella* story, *Camp Rock* chronicles the story of Mitchie Torres (Demi Lovato), who has a beautiful singing voice and dreams of becoming a pop singer. All she wants is the opportunity to spend the summer at a famous rock camp, but the camp is not cheap and Mitchie's family simply can't afford to send her there. However, her mother, Connie (Maria Canals Barrera), gets a job as Camp Rock's cook, giving Mitchie access to the camp just so long as she helps out in the kitchen. Mitchie strikes up a friendship with Caitlyn (Alyson Stoner), as well as the clique led by Tess Tyler (Meaghan Jette Martin). Complications arise as Mitchie pretends to be a wealthy camper so that she can fit in. She's overheard (but not seen) by Shane Gray (Joe Jonas), part of the pop superstar band Connect 3. He is fascinated by her voice and is determined to find out who the girl behind it is. Mitchie learns to be true to herself and be honest — even if might threaten her blossoming relationship with Shane. Kevin Jonas plays Jason and Nick plays Nate, the other two-thirds of Connect 3.

lot, and one of the best things about it was that we would always meet girls there. I had this crush at camp and I thought it would be a smooth move to ask her to go on a canoe ride. And while I was out in the canoe, it actually flipped over. I don't know how it happened; I think one of my friends was teasing me, because I was with a girl and she got up and got scared, so she fell in

Demi Lovato said of her character, Mitchie: "She's your typical girl next door, but she's vulnerable. She starts out very insecure and really just wants to fit in. She's kind of shy, she hasn't really opened up yet and shown her full colors. She gets tangled up in innocent lies and falls in love, then the secrets start to unfold. Throughout the movie you see her grow and progress into a butterfly, and it's great to see her really blossom. I think you'll be shocked by who she becomes by the end of the movie. I think it's fun to watch when there's a real arc for the character."

"My character, Shane, is a pop star who kind of loses his way and has to go back to his roots at Camp Rock," said Joe. "He's kind of a bit of a jerk, but you see him gradually grow out of that."

Added Kevin: "Shane gets a really big head on his shoulders and starts becoming like this ultimate diva — or divo — and we can't take it anymore. We're sending him back to Camp Rock to be a counselor and find himself. We even end up canceling our tour. So he goes back to Camp Rock and kind of starts the process of getting back to who he really is. You know, not caring about

brothers avoid going down the same kind of path that derails Shane. "I think it's cool, because we do this with each other and we are able to watch each other's back," he said, "and when somebody says something stupid, we're like, 'Psh, whatever.' It's funny to play that role, because it's not how we are in real life. I'm more the funny one in real life and for me to be kind of serious and all suave is kind of funny. It was a fun challenge."

For her part, Demi loved working with the Jonas Brothers. "You don't find three good, humble, classic gentleman rock stars — there's no such thing, you know what I mean?" she mused. "They're rock stars, but yet, when they get offstage, they're nerds and gentlemen, and they're, like, humble. Just great guys."

She's also pretty enthusiastic about shooting the film itself. "We shot in the Canadian countryside, like, 45 minutes from civilization," she said. "It was a beautiful place. We felt like we really were in camp." Joe shared that feeling, noting: "We felt like it *was* camp because for us we are so used to being so busy, being in one place for, like, a month was just almost surreal. We are so used to moving around so much that it felt like you are at camp. You are at this beautiful place, you woke up, you did activities, so it was like camp in that way."

the image, not caring about what people think of him, but more about the music and what the real meaning is."

"In the movie," Nick offered, "Shane needs to find his roots again, he meets Mitchie and while they are both trying to find themselves, they find each other as well. And it all comes back to just the music and how that really just changes everything and makes it all good again. It's a great story and the music is amazing. I think people are gonna love it."

Joe was asked by CNN how he and his

For Disney's Gary Marsh, the appeal of *Camp Rock* is simple: "If *High School Musical* was about following your dreams, this is about finding your voice."

The Cast of *Camp Rock*

Demi Lovato (Mitchie Torres)

As much as *Camp Rock* has been marketed as a Jonas Brothers movie, at its heart is Demi Lovato as Mitchie Torres. Shortly before the film aired, Demi started to realize that her career could be transformed by its success, possibly elevating her to the star status of Miley Cyrus or the Jonas Brothers themselves.

"There's definitely nervousness," she admitted, "even though I've been preparing myself for this career since I was eight and I've always been working towards this and wanting this, of course. Finally it's here and I'm *so* nervous. I thought I would be so used to it by now and it would be more like, 'Okay, I'm going to do this and that and a concert, and now I'm so nervous. Not nervous in a bad way, because I've been anticipating it, but when I look at Hannah Montana and the Jonas Brothers, who are on yogurts and magazines, I think it's awesome and I can't wait to hopefully be there, too.

"I think *Camp Rock* can be a defining moment for me in some ways," she added. "My favorite quote is 'Never believe the hype,' because you do a job and someone says, 'This is going to make you a star,' and then it doesn't. Hopefully it will work, but you just don't know."

One thing that Demi, who was born on August 20, 1992, in Dallas, Texas, *did* know was that she wanted a career in the enter-tainment world and it's something she began pursuing at a young age.

"I left public school in seventh grade to be home-schooled," she related. "The reason is that there were mean girls in this school. Girls can be very vicious and I was performing at the time, so it was hard for me to go to public school and keep up with the work. I'm not a huge fan of drama and I can't deal with it at all, and you know how middle school is. So I asked my mom if I could be home-schooled and she said okay. Selena Gomez, who's my best friend, was

really all I had, with the exception of my guitar and my piano. Whenever I would write, I could express so much and I guess that's when I realized that I can't live without this. It made me appreciate the art of guitar and piano and writing. I would do — and still do — my schoolwork for three hours a day, and then I would practice music and go to an acting class or something. It allowed me to develop my passion and my art. There are a lot of distractions at public school and this just fits me better."

Demi's first role came when she was six years old as she joined the cast of *Barney & Friends* (which is where she met *Wizard of Waverly Place*'s Selena Gomez). As time went on she scored guest-starring roles in

such shows as *Prison Break* and *Just Jordan*, as well as the pilot for *Split Ends*. Her first real connection with Disney came as Charlotte Adams in the series *As the Bell Rings*. Each episode only runs several minutes in length, serving as "bumpers" between different Disney Channel series. In addition to *Camp Rock* and its forthcoming sequel, she co-stars (with bestie Selena Gomez) in the 2009 Disney Channel movie *Princess Protection Program*. Also coming up for Demi is 2009's *Sonny with a Chance*, a Disney comedy series about a Wisconsin teenage girl named Sonny (played by Demi) who moves to Los Angeles after being cast in her favorite teen sketch comedy show called *So Random*. *Sonny* is about the effect that

feel of going on tour, waking up in the middle of the night and continually moving to a different city. We wrote about 10 really good songs and we're excited about them. Some days I would have an idea on piano and we'd start writing the chords. Everyone had an equal amount of input, which was awesome. It's not like two people are writing and someone punches in a line. It was a real collaboration and I don't think I've ever experienced anything like that. It was awesome. I love writing with them and they're so completely professional."

Produced by John Fields, who also produced the Jonas Brothers albums *Jonas Brothers* and *A Little Bit Longer*, the album was tracked in 10 days. Demi wrote or co-wrote all but two of the 11 songs on the album, and the Jonas Brothers co-wrote six of those nine songs. "I tend to write songs that are, I guess, a little bit more intense and less catchy, and I needed help writing catchy songs," she related to MTV. "So that's where they came in. I put a lot of my musical input and lyrics into these songs, and they just helped me with hooks and stuff like that.... It's my first one, so I wanted it to be fun — stuff you can drive around in your car to and jam out to."

"It's got a lot of messages that I wanted to get out. I want people to hear one song about feeling insecure and not always feeling beautiful," she told *OK Magazine*. "That's one song that I hope girls will relate to. You are beautiful." On October 1, 2008, Demi appeared on *Ellen* and talked about being

move has on her life, and features the sketches from the show-within-the-show.

But acting is not all Demi can do. 2008 saw her recording career take off too. On September 23, her debut album, *Don't Forget*, was released and hit the #2 spot on the *Billboard* 200 chart.

"I wrote it with [the Jonas Brothers]," she explained. "I went on tour with them for two or three weeks and we wrote songs together. They wanted me to get used to the

bullied in the seventh grade, and how she wants to help other girls deal with bullying.

The Jonas Brothers helped Demi out with more than just songwriting. "Take the high road," she said they advised. "I've learned that from the boys — the Jonas Brothers — and two wrongs don't make a right. They really help me out with the things I'm going through."

On the day of the album's release, the JoBros wrote on their blog: "Just wanted to let you know that Demi's new CD is in stores TODAY!!! We are so proud of our friend. She is an amazing singer and musician. Also, we want you to know that we were able to co-write and co-produce 6 of the songs on the CD. There is even a duet we can't wait for you to hear." That duet is the fifth track on the album, "On the Line." In addition to being great friends with the Jonas Brothers, Demi also shares their management team: Kevin Jonas Sr. and Philip McIntyre of The Jonas Group, as well as Eddie De La Garza for De La Garza Entertainment.

Demi only did a limited number of concerts to support the album, because she was busy shooting her new series *Sonny with a Chance*, but she did get to be the opening act for the Jonas Brothers on their Burning Up tour.

Demi was actually a part of their previous tour (Look Me in the Eyes) as well, but not in a singing capacity. "I actually would go on stage and introduce them," she said, "and *that* was mind-blowing. To walk out in front of thousands of people and stand on the stage — even though I wasn't singing — just holding a microphone and standing on stage in front of all of those people was incredible. . . . I came away having had an awesome experience and eagerness to hopefully one day go on tour."

Looking to the future, Demi has definite goals in mind: "In the next couple of years — well, I haven't really been able to do a lot of music, because I've been acting. I would really like to make [more] albums, rock out, have fun at the Disney Channel and when I'm a little older start working on more serious films and character roles. Maybe a scary movie or something. But for the moment, I'm just having fun and enjoying myself."

Meaghan Jette Martin
(Tess Tyler)

Any good drama has a balance between good and evil, and that's true in *Camp Rock*. Demi Lovato's Mitchie Torres is the "good girl" while Meaghan Jette Martin's Tess Tyler represents the dark side. The thing that makes this dynamic realistic is that as difficult as Tess makes Mitchie's life at camp, there is another side to her which explains her actions . . . to some degree.

"Tess is incredibly evil and nobody likes her," admitted her real-life alter ego. "But they're all so afraid of her that they pretend to like her, and she always gets her way. But she doesn't have the best home life, so it's kind of explained why she's so evil.

"In some ways it was hard to play some-

one so mean and at the same time it wasn't. The hardest part was to have to be mean to these people that I was getting so close to in the movie. We were all becoming best friends and, you know, the director would call, 'Action!' and I would have to yell at them. So that wasn't so much fun. But the entire cast was great, and I mean, they knew I was acting. And it was good to play a character that I like to think isn't like me — hopefully I'm nothing like her."

Born on February 17, 1992, in Las Vegas, Nevada, Meaghan, who has two solo songs in *Camp Rock*, scored her first role in the form of voiceover work in 1999's *Dog Boy*. She's appeared in a number of stage productions, among them 2002's *Grease* (as Patty Simcox), 2003's *Sleeping Beauty* (as the young version of the title character), 2004's *Schoolhouse Rock Live!* (as a lead soloist), 2005's *A Christmas Carol* (as Carol Cratchit and Elizabeth), and 2006's *The Wind in the Willows* (as Ratty), *13* (as Kendra) and *Dorothy Meets Alice* (as Alice).

Her TV credits include 2006's *Cookin' Rocks*, 2007's *Close to Home* and *The Suite Life of Zack and Cody* and a guest spot on *House* in 2008. Among her feature credits are 2008's *Camp Rock* and *Privileged*, and 2009's *Camp Rock 2* and *Dear Lemon Lima*.

Not surprisingly, given her singing in *Camp Rock*, Meaghan is working on her first CD. "It's more of a pop/rock sound," she detailed, "but the producer I'm working with is very open to me using my Broadway style, because vocally, when I sing, you can

Alyson Stoner and Meaghan Jette Martin pose at the premiere of *Camp Rock* in New York City.

when Caitlyn discovers that Mitchie lied. But friendship wins out in the end.

"Caitlyn is an aspiring music producer," said Alyson. "Fashion-wise, she mixes and matches a bunch of crazy color with what she wears every day. She befriends Mitchie, but she unfortunately watches Mitchie fall into the trap of the mean girl. So, she's very sarcastic, funky and kind of creative, I'd say. She's an artist. In real life, I actually do compose my own music at home on my electronic keyboard and computer. So, that's definitely a similarity between the two of us, but I'm not as confident.

"What I do like about her," Alyson continued, "is that for her, nothing is too much. The more the better — that's Caitlyn's motto. She mixes and matches clothes that I could never imagine wearing, but somehow I always got compliments on set for my outfits. She has an eye for color schemes. Being able to pull off all these colors is something I've always wanted to be able to do, so I got to on set."

Born on August 11, 1993, in Toledo, Ohio, Alyson's first love has always been dancing and, following extensive choreography training, she scored background dancing roles in a number of music videos, including Eminem's "Just Lose It" and Missy Elliott's "Gossip Folks" and "Work It." Between the years 2003 and 2006, she was part of a dancing group called the JammXKids.

In explaining what draws her to dance, Alyson related: "There's absolutely every

hear that I have a Broadway voice. He's very accepting of that and he likes it, so we're really working on that. And I would absolutely love to be in a Broadway show someday. That's always been my goal, just be in a Broadway show. Only one, that's what I'm asking for."

Alyson Stoner (Caitlyn Gellar)

The one true friend that Mitchie finds at Camp Rock is Alyson Stoner's Caitlyn Gellar — and even they have problems

kind of song and every kind of move you can do to express every emotion. If you're sad, you can do this; if you're happy, you can do that. The possibilities are endless. You can be creative and just be who you want to be, and that's what I love about choreography. I can design my own dances to fit my personality, rather than following someone else's."

She was also drawn to acting, and got her first big break as a co-host of *Mike's Super Short Show* on the Disney Channel, a gig that lasted from 2002 to 2006. She portrayed Sarah Baker in 2003's *Cheaper By the Dozen* and its 2005 sequel, provided the voice for "Kid Rat" in 2004's *Garfield* and was Camille in 2007's *Step Up*. On the small screen she guest starred on *Drake & Josh*, *I'm With Her*, *The Suite Life of Zack and Cody*, *That's So Raven* and *Joey*. She also starred in the TV movie *Alice Down Under* and provided her voice to *Lilo & Stitch: The Series*, *W.I.T.C.H.* and *Phineas and Ferb*. In 2008, Alyson launched *The Alyson Stoner Project*, a "dance video hybrid," which included dance instruction as well as fan-created content from an online dance contest.

Like many of her *Camp Rock* co-stars, Alyson is interested in pursuing singing. "I've had to sing for different jobs in my character voice for animated series," she explained. "I wanted to explore singing as myself. I began training vocally about a year-and-a-half ago. From there, I've been writing music. My love for music is extremely strong, because I'm a dancer. It's

fairly new to me, but I feel like it's been there my whole life. I'm ready to take off and pursue that whole area." She described her sound as a "soulful pop vibe with a little alternative edge."

Anna Maria Perez de Tagle (Ella)

One of Tess's followers is Anna Maria Perez de Tagle's Ella, a character who, like the others, will be returning for *Camp Rock 2*.

For the actress, *Camp Rock* represented something of a reunion. "I met Demi on a show called *Just Jordan*," she explained. "Ever since then we kept in touch. She visited me on the set of *Hannah Montana* and we switched phone numbers. And then, all of a sudden, we were like, 'We're going to be on *Camp Rock*.'"

"Ella is the girlie girl of the mean clique," she added about her character, "and she's kind of obsessed with lip gloss, most of all. She's obsessed with her lip gloss, her makeup, her clothes, her hair. She's not the sharpest tool in the shed. She's kind of ditzy at times. But her character changes towards the end of the movie, so that's kind of cool. She was always fun to play. It's kind of funny, because I actually play this type of character on *Hannah Montana* also, so it was always a lot of fun and kind of familiar to me. It's always fun to play the mean girl."

Born on December 23, 1990, in San Francisco, California, she actually didn't start pursuing a career in acting until she graduated from high school, at which point she moved to southern California, where she was soon cast in the recurring role of Ashley Dewitt on *Hannah Montana*, a character who serves as an adversary of sorts for Miley Stewart. She also appeared on the shows *Higglytown Heroes* and *Just Jordan*. On the big screen, fans can find her in *Bleachers*, *A Forgotten Innocence* and *Hannah Montana: The Movie*.

Anna Maria is quick to point out that she is pleased with the message of *Camp Rock*: "I think people relate to this movie a lot just because there are morals — like, to always be yourself and never be somebody you're not. That kind of happens in the movie, and I think that will totally translate to the audience and the kids who are watching it."

Jasmine Richards
(Margaret "Peggy" Dupree)

Camp Rock's "axis of evil" is rounded off with Jasmine Richards' Peggy, who pretty much follows Tess's lead. Born on June 28, 1990, in Scarborough, Ontario, Jasmine's acting roles have included 2003's *Time-blazers*, 2005's *Devotion*, a supporting role in *Naturally Sadie* from 2005 to 2007, 2007's *da Kink in My Hair* and the TV pilot

Overruled!, 2008's TV movie *Princess* and, of course, *Camp Rock*.

"The most challenging part of my job," she related, "would be waking up in the morning. I have no problems getting into character or learning my lines, but when it comes to actually waking up early in the morning to go to work, it seems to be the hardest for me. I like my sleep, what can I say? I also have to say that seeing myself on TV is weird. Sometimes I flip through the channels, and all of a sudden I'll see my face pop up. I don't think it will ever become a normal thing to me."

The Soundtrack

Not surprisingly given the Jonas Brothers' presence on it, the soundtrack to *Camp Rock* was a significant hit. Not only did it reach #2 on the iTunes store, but it debuted at #3 on the *Billboard* 200 with 188,000 copies sold in its first week. Ultimately the disc sold over 1 million copies.

The track breakdown on the album is: "We Rock" (the cast), "Play My Music" (Connect 3/Jonas Brothers), "Gotta Find You" (Shane/Joe Jonas), "Start the Party" (Barron/Jordan Francis), "Who Will I Be?" (Mitchie/Demi Lovato), "This is Me" (Mitchie/Demi Lovato and Shane/Joe Jonas), "Hasta La Vista" (Barron/Jordan Francis and Ella/Anna Maria Perez de Tagle), "Here I Am" (Peggy/Jasmine Richards), "Too Cool" (Tess/Meaghan Jette Martin), "Our Time is Here" (Mitchie/Demi Lovato, Tess/Meaghan Jette Martin and Lola/Aaryn Doyle), "2 Stars" (Tess/Meaghan Jette Martin) and "What It Takes" (Lola/Aaryn Doyle).

Camp Rock Hits

While the cast was hopeful that *Camp Rock* would be a hit, everyone involved was caught off guard by the fan frenzy that hit New York's Ziegfeld Theatre on June 12, 2008, when Disney hosted its premiere with all the glitz of a feature film release.

Admitted Joe, "Tonight is very exciting for us. New York really turned out to embrace us." "It's our first movie," added Kevin, "so we're just truly honored to be able to be here. We're really excited."

Enthused Demi, "It feels incredible; it feels like a dream. I didn't know I had that many fans. I looked up as they screamed my name and I was like, 'Cool. You know my name!'" Thanks to *Camp Rock*, everybody seemed to know Demi's name, and many of the movie's reviews had great things to say about her and her co-stars.

"Mitchie is adorable," said the *Corpus Christi Caller-Times*, "with a huge Mary Lou Retton smile. Joe Jonas has the shaggy rock musician look down and is, according to teen girls, 'hot, hot, hot!' Cue the music, which is actually good but rather overproduced. . . . The dancing is also good, but the movie's best feature is that it highlights a romance that doesn't even include kissing."

The *Chicago Sun-Times* pointed to *Camp Rock*'s "not-so-secret weapon — the squeaky-clean pop band the Jonas Brothers

… While the focus of the film is on Joe, both Nick and Kevin manage to steal a few scenes here and there, and the brothers of course perform a song or two, which should delight their legion of fans … The music is cut from the same cloth as tunes from *High School Musical*. Many of the songs have pop hooks that will have some fans humming along."

The *New York Post* was surprisingly positive in their look at the film: "*Camp Rock* concerns itself with the same issues you might encounter in a made-for-TV musical about a high school, mainly how to fit in while also maintaining one's individuality. It's a really great movie, like a modern-day version of an old Judy Garland–Mickey Rooney picture in which the kids put on a show that improves the lives of all who see it. Watching this movie yesterday was one of the most pleasant afternoons I have spent recently doing this job that all kids envy."

"This is a hit," proclaimed the *Miami Herald*, "and has been carefully crafted by Disney to become one. The formula may be as old as pop culture itself, but who really cares? Formulas shouldn't necessarily earn demerits because they are formulas; what counts is how cleverly or skillfully the creators have worked within the confines. Here they've worked perfectly well."

Said the New York *Daily News*: "*Camp Rock* may be specifically designed to ride on the success of *High School Musical*, but its formula goes back to the animated Disney classics of decades past: a vulnerable heroine, a villain, a white knight, a crisis and,

well, you get the idea. This is *Cinderella* or *Snow White* in contemporary casual with a z-100 beat."

The positive responses combined with Disney's promotional push turned *Camp Rock* into an unquestionable hit. The film, which made its Disney Channel debut on June 20, 2008 (and which, incidentally, cost $15 million — three times the cost of the first *High School Musical*) enjoyed solid ratings in its initial roll out. On the 20th, it reached nearly 9 million viewers on the Disney Channel and nearly 1 million on Canada's Family Channel; on the 21st, it aired on ABC to an audience of 3.5 million viewers; on the 22nd, it was broadcast on ABC Family to nearly 4 million viewers. On the 23rd, the film was webcast on Disney.com, reaching 863,000 more people.

Camp Rock didn't just reach audiences in North America; it was broadcast in Latin America, Japan and other Asian countries, Italy, Portugal, the U.K. and Ireland, Germany, Austria, Spain, France, New Zealand, Australia and in the Middle East over course of the summer and into the fall.

Wasting little time, Disney also issued *Camp Rock* on DVD and Blu-Ray on August 19. Extras on the disc include: an extended ending; sing-along and karaoke functions; the featurettes "How to Be a Rock Star," "Jonas Brothers: Real Life Rock Stars," "Introducing Demi Lovato," "Too Cool: Setting the Stage" and "Hasta La Vista: From Rehearsal to Final Jam"; as well as music videos and "Camp Memories," a photo gallery.

Camp Rock: The Story Continues

For anyone who simply can't get enough of *Camp Rock*, Disney launched a line of books. *Camp Rock: The Junior Novel* (May 2008) is a novelization of the film but original stories appear in the *Camp Rock Second Session Series*. In *Play it Again* (September 2008), a new guy tries to win Mitchie's affection and in the second book, *The Record* (September 2008), Tess tries to land a recording contract. *Going Platinum* (November 2008), the third in the series, features a plot about Shane and Mitchie dealing with the return of a girl from Shane's past. A scavenger hunt to win a guest spot on Connect 3's new album has Mitchie and Caitlyn teaming up in *Hidden Tracks* (January 2009). Tess's superstar mom shows up at Camp Rock in *Rock Royalty* (March 2009) and Mitchie imagines how the other half lives.

And the story will continue on screen as well as in books, with a sequel to *Camp Rock* planned. In the weeks before *Camp Rock* actually aired, Disney could feel the growing interest on the part of the fans, which was no doubt fueled by the increasing popularity of the Jonas Brothers. Mused Disney's Gary Marsh, "It feels like some giant wave forming out on the ocean. You don't know how big it's going to be until it hits."

Well, hit it did and plans are fully underway for a summer 2009 broadcast of *Camp Rock 2*. Reported the online Disney Society last June, "Filming of the movie won't begin until early 2009. The Jonas Brothers will each share equal time in the sequel . . . and the 'Bonus Jonas,' their little brother Frankie, will make an appearance also." While the details of the plot are kept under wraps, the cast will all be back at Camp Rock . . . once the Jonas Brothers and Demi Lovato have some free time in their schedules to film it!

Real-Life Rock Camps

Rock camps are becoming increasingly popular all over the world, providing a fantastic training ground for aspiring musicians. Camps generally run about a week, where kids can hone their skills on the guitar, bass, keyboard or drums. Campers form their own bands, practice together, write their own music, and sometimes even record their own CD! Usually the camps finish with a live show, in which the new rockers can showcase their skills. Some camps also cover rock history, so that the budding stars can learn about the successes of the past and identify their musical influences. Rock camps are popping up all over the place — with Camp Jam in 18 cities, and other prominent rock camps in Austin, Chicago and Portland.

Rock camps just for girls are also becoming increasingly popular, and got a lot of attention with the 2007 documentary *Girls Rock*. *Girls Rock* follows four girls between the ages of 8 and 18 at the Rock 'n' Roll Camp for Girls in Portland, Oregon. At the Rock 'n' Roll Camp, girls are encouraged to express themselves with voice, music and movement, setting themselves free of the daily pressures of being young women. The camp's main message is that "it is 100% okay to be exactly who you are" — a message perfectly in tune with the spirit of *Camp Rock*. Other camps just for rockin' girls can be found in Brooklyn, Murfreesboro, Philadelphia, Austin, Washington and even England and Sweden.

Want to be on stage but not sure rock is for you? There are also plenty of performing arts camps across the country. The Jonas Brothers' Change for the Children Foundation supports one in particular: the Summer Stars Camp for the Performing Arts in Northfield, Massachusetts. At Summer Stars Camp, kids between 12 and 15 take classes in dance, drumming, juggling, improvisational acting, choral singing, blues performance, set design, musical theater and music video production. What makes the camp unique is that it's only for economically disadvantaged kids, who can attend for free thanks to donors like the Jonas Brothers. With new rock and performance camps opening all the time, it's pretty safe to say summer camp isn't just for crafts and canoeing anymore.

Chapter 18

JoBros TV

From the moment they signed with Disney, TV and the Jonas Brothers have gone hand-in-hand. It began with their music videos airing on the Disney Channel, which instantly increased their fan base, brought more awareness of their music and, really, introduced them to the world in a major way. The videos were followed by a guest starring appearance on the *Hannah Montana* episode "Me and Mr. Jonas and Mr. Jonas and Mr. Jonas," and, of course, the summer '08 hit, *Camp Rock*.

But beyond all of this, Disney has been working behind the scenes to turn Kevin, Nick and Joe into bonafide television stars, beginning with the pilot for *J.O.N.A.S.* (*Junior Operatives Networking As Spies*). Unlike most Disney Channel series fare, which is shot on tape in front of a studio audience, the plan for *J.O.N.A.S.* was to film it on out-of-studio locations as well as in different studio-built sets.

The original idea for the show, as Joe explained during the time of the pilot's production, was "we're government agents. The bad guys are always trying to take over the teen world and our cover is that we're a band, the Jonas Brothers, and our mission is to stop them. People on the show know us as a band who have started to make it in the music industry, but we leave a concert to stop a villain who's trying to destroy the world."

Added Kevin: "It's definitely fun and very *Austin Powers*–ish. I also think it's a little more mature than some of the other shows on the Disney Channel, and being a single-camera show [meaning it's shot like a movie or dramatic series], it gives us amazing opportunities to try different things. When this subject first came up, we told them that we didn't want the show to be cheesy. We wanted there to be stunts and for the episodes to be action-packed."

Besides *Austin Powers*, Joe felt the pilot incorporated the feel of things like *The Monkees* and James Bond. "It's *really* funny," he said at the time. "When we were watching it, we got so caught up that we were laughing like we'd forgotten we were in it. Shooting the pilot was the greatest experience ever, and the single camera approach is exactly what we wanted. Having a laugh track is great, but this gives people the opportunity to laugh for themselves. It doesn't feel like somebody is laughing for you. We had such a great time, because we were able to do so much. We could film things outside and we could have huge tour buses in the shot. It was so amazing and cool."

Actress Chelsea Staub (whose credits include roles on *Wizards of Waverly Place*, *That's So Raven*, *Even Stevens* and the TV movie *Minutemen*) was cast as a co-star in *J.O.N.A.S.* "I'm this writer for a teen magazine," she explained of her character, "who doesn't realize they're spies, but I go on dates with all three of them without them knowing that I'm dating the other brothers, and I write about it in my column. And they have no idea where this information is coming from. So pretty much the entire show,

it's all of us lying to each other and kind of everything backfiring and us getting caught in awkward situations. It's really funny . . . and a little confusing."

One thing that Chelsea was preparing herself for was fans who would get jealous over her "dating" the Jonas Brothers. "I'm a little nervous," she admitted. "The Jonas Brothers have some pretty crazy fans. They're great, though. Their fans are so cool. They're so supportive of the boys, and the boys are just the nicest things you'll ever meet. They're so sweet. And I just hope the girls realize that I love the Jonas Brothers as much as they do. And I'm a fan, too, and I'm not out to 'steal' any of them or something like that. I'm actually really excited to be in a show with guys that already have such a big fan base. It's like, 'Wow, lucky me that I get to kind of fall into that.'"

Joe believed that *J.O.N.A.S.* would definitely be a show for all ages, with him imagining parents rushing home from work while kids are rushing home from school to make sure they have their popcorn so they can enjoy the show together.

"It's definitely really cool," he pointed out, "because there's a lot of action stuff and fighting — we had to undergo kung fu training for it. Growing up with shows like *Even Stevens* — and now Shia LaBeouf is one of the biggest stars in Hollywood. We always said that a show we did should be like that one where you can film in different places. Shows like *The Suite Life of Zack and Cody* are restricted to their sets. With our show, we can build different sets every day. We had a big warehouse and they would build a school in it one day. Then the next day they would knock it down and build an evil lair. It's just unbelievable."

"We went through a week and a half of martial arts training to get ready for the pilot," Kevin said. "We had to do stunts. We were on cables and all that kind of stuff, and it was absolutely awesome. We actually trained with a guy named Koichi Sakamoto. He's the man who trained the Power Rangers, which was exciting for us."

Enthused Nick, "What we love about it is that it's just a really cool concept. It's got an amazing, unique feel to it and it feels a lot different from everything else that's out there. And it's a great opportunity for us to play exaggerated versions of ourselves."

Well, as things have turned out, the exaggerated versions of themselves will *not* be the Jonas Brothers as spies. The decision was made to alter the premise of *J.O.N.A.S.* The original pilot reportedly tested quite well and Disney seemed ready to go forward with the series itself, but then things got hung up. The premise was going through some tweaks before production got underway, but then word came out that the show wasn't going to happen at all — the guys would be starring in a completely different series.

Long-time Jonas family friends Kiyoko (a.k.a. Coach K) and Maya join Frankie and Joe on set.

with their personal life. They'll be living with their parents (played by actors rather than their actual mother and father) and brother Frankie in a New Jersey fire station (but the show is filmed in L.A.). According to reports, actor John Ducey will play their on-screen father, and head of security Big Rob will have a recurring role (presumably as their bodyguard). Actress Nicole Anderson (whose credits include *iCarly*, *Hannah Montana* and *Zoey 101*) will play their biggest fan at school, whose presence means that something odd will ultimately happen. And Chelsea Staub is still a key member of the cast.

Richard Huff of the New York *Daily News* provided a few more details: "The brothers will live in an old firehouse converted into a home, meaning they'll have a fire pole to go floor to floor. The house will have vending machines packed with healthy snacks . . . A couple of story lines to whet Jonas fans' appetites: In one, Joe falls for a girl who plays cello in the school orchestra and won't date a rock star. So he joins the orchestra. In another, all three have a crush on a pizza delivery girl, so they keep ordering pizzas over and over." In November 2008, shortly after filming got underway, EW.com revealed a still from an episode where the brothers light their kitchen on fire trying to bake a birthday cake for their mom.

Joe revealed in an interview, "It's going to be about us as a band, but dealing with normal things, like trying to take out the

It's not a great a leap of imagination to think that the studio took a cue from *Hannah Montana* in reimagining the show. Instead of featuring the boys as spies, *JONAS* now presents a thinly veiled version of Kevin, Nick and Joe as the Lucas brothers, who are trying to balance their stage life

trash and not get hounded by fans. It's going to be a funny show and it's going to be a great cast. . . . I'm really excited."

By the time that *JONAS* airs in 2009, Nick, Joe and Kevin will have already proven themselves to be seasoned vets in front of the camera. The real question is whether or not they're concerned about getting tied down to a TV series at this stage in their career.

"Not a big worry," said Joe, "because of how perfectly it ties into our music and focuses on us as being musicians. A lot of folks like to keep their music and acting separate, but we feel if you're going to do both, you might as well do them together."

The JoBros were also excited about their summer 2008 Disney Channel reality series, *Jonas Brothers: Living the Dream*, which brought their fans a little closer to their world by going behind the scenes of their Look Me in the Eyes tour.

Disney recognized that the fans would love to get an inside look at the making of this tour, so they following the guys around with cameras while they rehearsed, performed on stage and as they went about their personal lives. As Kevin noted, "This isn't a typical reality show where they're editing stories together. This is our daily life and they're capturing it on film."

As the guys explained on radio station Hot 99.5, "There's going to be a lot of

A lot of folks like to keep their music and acting separate, but we feel if you're going to do both, you might as well do them together.

footage that is really fun. You're going to see our life on tour. The early mornings, late nights, to the fun times we have on the road, go-carting, indoor skydiving, playing a concert every night. It's going to be a really funny show."

The show, each episode of which was narrated by a different Jonas, ran from May 16, 2008, to September 5, 2008.

Episode 1: "To-Do List"
Narrated by Nick
Original Airdate: May 16, 2008
Starting right at the beginning of the tour, the episode shows how the entire Jonas clan (including the boys' parents and little brother Frankie) prepare to leave home and get started on an extended "road trip."

Episode 2: "The Big Game"
Narrated by Kevin
Original Airdate: May 23, 2008
Arriving in Tucson, Arizona, the guys check out the stage they'll be performing on, and then begin the rehearsal process.

Episode 3: "Downtime"
Narrated by Joe
Original Airdate: May 30, 2008
So, what do you do when you're as famous and rich as the Jonas Brothers and you've got a little bit of free time on your schedule? If you're Kevin, Joe, Nick and Frankie, you give indoor skydiving a shot.

Episode 4: "Our Fans Rock"
Narrated by Kevin
Original Airdate: June 6, 2008
What starts off as a meeting with a large group of fans turns into a surprise concert while the guys are in Tucson, Arizona.

Episode 5: "Driver's Ed"
Narrated by Joe
Original Airdate: June 13, 2008
The Jonases have moved on in their journey, arriving in Salt Lake City, Utah (where, incidentally, *High School Musical* was filmed). Finding himself with a little bit of down time, Joe, accompanied by the rest of his family, decides to take some driving lessons.

Episode 6: "Our Mom and Dad"
Narrated by Joe
Original Airdate: June 27, 2008
Focusing pretty firmly on Kevin Sr. and Denise, this particular episode demonstrates the challenges the Jonas parents have in keeping their kids grounded when everything else in their world seems to have gone so absolutely crazy.

Episode 7: "Hello Hollywood"
Narrated by Joe
Original Airdate: July 4, 2008
For Nick, Kevin and Joe, playing a concert in Hollywood is just about the best: awesome fans, being in their new hometown, all their Disney friends at the show and a post-concert bowling competition!

Episode 8: "Health Kick"
Narrated by Joe
Original Airdate: July 11, 2008
Living the kind of life that they do — one that seldom gives them the chance to slow down — has to take a physical toll on the guys, and this episode shows how they eat and work out to stay healthy and in shape for their hectic lifestyle.

Episode 9: "We Are Family"
Narrated by Kevin
Original Airdate: July 18, 2008
By now fans are familiar with the immediate Jonas fam — Nick, Joe, Kevin, Frankie, Kevin Sr. and Denise — but this episode introduces the extended members of the JoBros family.

Episode 10: "School Rocks"
Narrated by Nick
Original Airdate: July 25, 2008
Education waits for no superstar: Nick balances his studies with his life as a part of the Jonas Brothers, going on a field trip to a Titanic museum.

Taylor Swift joins Joe on stage to perform "Should've Said No" for the 3D concert movie.

Episode 11: "Musical Scrapbook"
Narrated by Nick
Original Airdate: August 1, 2008
For fans, this one must have been an ultimate "insider's look"; the guys reveal how they write songs together, and discuss the inspiration for their lyrics.

Episode 12: "Nothing's Gonna Slow Me Down"
Narrated by Nick
Original Airdate: August 8, 2008
Definitely a more serious theme, Nick shares with fans how he manages to control his diabetes despite being on the road so much of the time.

Episode 14: "We're the Boss"
Narrated by Kevin
Original Airdate: August 29, 2008
For anyone who thought the Jonas Brothers were being controlled by others, this episode is an eye-opener. The guys are very much in charge of their own affairs, as they detail here.

Episode 15: "Dream On"
Narrated by Kevin
Original Airdate: September 5, 2008
For the Jonas Brothers everything comes full circle as they bring their tour to a close by playing a show in their former home state, New Jersey.

Not limiting themselves to just the small screen, the Jonas Brothers followed in label-mate Miley Cyrus's footsteps and filmed two concerts on their Burning Up tour to turn into a 3D concert film. *Jonas Brothers: The 3D Concert Experience* featured the Jonas Brothers performing on July 13 and 14, 2008, in Anaheim, California, as well as tons of backstage and bonus footage and performances by Taylor Swift and Demi Lovato. Released on February 27, 2009, *Jonas Brothers: The 3D Concert Experience* was just the first time the brothers Jonas would hit the big screen; in October 2008, *Variety* broke the news that they would be appearing in the film adaptation of *Walter the Farting Dog* along with Frankie.

It's a JoBros hot-dog stand! Kevin and Taylor Swift film a scene for the 3D movie in New York City.

Episode 13: "Rock Star in Training"
Narrated by Nick
Original Airdate: August 15, 2008
The Bonus Jonas hits the spotlight in this Frankie-centric episode, allowing viewers to get to know the littlest Jonas better.

Chapter 19

A Little Bit Longer

Oftentimes when you look at a band that's at the top of its game — who seem to be everywhere at once — you can't help but wonder how the heck they ever had time to record a new album. There simply doesn't seem to be enough hours in a day to get it all done, especially when you consider the maddening schedule that the Jonas Brothers keep.

Apparently the guys recognized the same challenge themselves, but rather than give up touring or recording, they decided to do *both*, with the help of Gibson Guitar, which was supplying their tour bus. Explained Kevin, "We approached Gibson and said,

'What can you do to help us?' Our goal is to never stop and get it while it's hot."

The solution was to turn the tour bus into a mobile recording studio so that Kevin, Joe and Nick could record, working with returning producer John Fields between gigs. Noted Gibson's CEO Henry Juszkiewicz, "Band in a Bus was such a unique idea and perfect for our state-of-the-art Gibson tour bus. We've been with the Jonas Brothers since the beginning and couldn't be happier about their success."

While Hollywood Records' Jon Lind admitted "the bus thing isn't necessarily ideal," he also acknowledged that "the guys

are in the absolute most creative period of their careers." Jonas Brothers co-manager Phil McIntyre offered, "We outfitted the tour bus with all the technology we would need and drove from city to city, laying down what would be the next record."

As Fields reflected to *Mix*, "We set up shop at Cherry Beach [studio] to cut what became the first five songs on this album. We needed a bunch more and we'd have a record, but they were on the Hannah Montana tour. They asked if I'd go on tour with them, and I said, 'In what capacity? And when?' They said, 'To cut new songs; we're thinking about getting a tour bus from Gibson to use as a mobile studio.' I knew I would not be able to do what I normally do and that I would be limited to guitars and little dinky keyboard sounds, but it was refreshing to use new stuff and get fresh sounds." And the boys decided to share the recording process with their fans by making an online web series, *Band in a Bus*, to document their journey.

That all sounds promising from a technical standpoint, but what about the music itself? "I think we've gotten a little better as musicians," Nick opined, "so maybe the chords of the songs are a little different, more mature. But it's still fun, pop/rock

music and lyrics. I think it's the same Jonas Brothers sound, but with just a couple more influences. We have some more Elvis Costello–type influences on it. There's a song called 'BB Good' which is definitely an Animals, Rascals type of influence and obviously, of course, the Beatles. I also think the lyrical content has gotten a little more in-depth as far as who we are as people and our personal lives, with our dating and all that, things we've gone through in the past year. We were really able to put it into song and make it a really cool record.

"So the songwriting is maturing as far as chord structure, but not lyrical content —

we're not drifting off into the abyss. We're just the same guys writing about the same type of things we've been writing about, but we've really kind of tried to expand our horizons when it comes to the style of music and all that. I think it's a good continuation of the last record, but just full of a lot of songs, personal experiences and things that we've gone through."

"We're laying down the basics for a great record," said Kevin. "It's going to be a fun record. Everyone keeps asking us, 'What's the attitude? What should we be looking for?' I'd say it's a hopeful, good-time kind of record. It brings a smile to our faces. And as

for it being recorded while we were touring, it won't suffer, because we believe in the songs we're writing. I think for us, since we're there from the beginning with the writing of the songs through the production, it just becomes a different experience. This music really is us. It's not, like, a manufactured version. It's really truly us and we hope people will have a totally different take on us as a band."

"We're thrilled with this record," Joe emphasized. "It's kind of a continuation of the last one. It's definitely not a completely different change in any means, but this record has definitely been inspired by some

> **This music really is us.**
> **It's not, like,**
> **a manufactured version.**

of the artists we look up to. We're very thrilled for the audience to hear it."

Interviewed by ABC, the guys were asked whether or not the songwriting process had changed for them. "We all write the songs together," Nick said. "I've written a couple on my own, but I think for us, songwriting and being really part of our music is one of our big passions. We really draw from personal experiences and things we've gone through, so a song like 'A Little Bit Longer' is actually about my diabetes. That was a song that I wrote, and to see that it went to number one in a day was amazing!"

A Little Bit Longer was released on August 12, debuting at #1 on the *Billboard* 200, and moving a total of 525,402 copies in its first week. Impressively, the album had #1 debuts on the Top Digital Albums, Top Internet Albums, Tastemakers and *Billboard* Comprehensive Albums charts. Week two saw the disc staying atop the *Billboard* 200, while it dropped to #4 in week three. Ultimately the album was certified platinum and gold in nations around the world. One

other pretty amazing figure: in its first week of release, not only was *A Little Bit Longer* #1, but the soundtrack to *Camp Rock* was #8 and their self-titled second album had risen to #10 — the first time an artist held three slots in the Nielsen SoundScan top 10. To promote the then-upcoming album, the boys hit the road on their North American Burning Up tour on July 4, 2008, with Demi Lovato opening for them.

Depending on where fans picked up the album, the bonus tracks were a little bit different. The album's main track listing was: "BB Good," "Burnin' Up," (which featured bodyguard Big Rob), "Shelf," "One Man Show," "Lovebug" (the album's second single), "Tonight," "Can't Have You," "Video Girl," "Pushin' Me Away," "Sorry," "Got Me Going Crazy" and "A Little Bit Longer." Fans who bought the album at Wal-Mart got "Live to Party" as a bonus track while the Target disc featured the Beatles classic "Hello Goodbye," which the Jonas Brothers were heard singing in TV commercials for the department store. The release of the album in Britain saw the bonus tracks "When You Look Me in the Eyes," "Live to Party" and a live version of "A Little Bit Longer."

The critics, of course, were quick to weigh in on the disc. Noted the *San*

Francisco Chronicle, "Drawing on unexpected influences such as Elvis Costello and Fountains of Wayne, it's dominated by '80s-leaning power pop songs such as 'BB Good,' 'Shelf' and 'Video Girl.' Front man Joe has a pleasantly raspy voice, and the band somehow manages to steer clear of syrupy ballads you might normally associate with a Disney-sanctioned act of Christian rockers."

"The Jonases seem to deserve a bit more credit than the rest of the Disney pinup crew," added the *Winnipeg Sun*. "They write the vast majority of their material and, believe it or not, draw more on the classic power-pop sounds of Cheap Trick and Fountains of Wayne than the sugary bubblegum you'd expect."

Enthused *USA Today*, "The Jonases fancy themselves rockers, and their riffing adds a welcome heft to their effervescent pop tunes. Pandemically infectious songs such as 'Shelf,' 'Tonight' and 'Pushin' Me Away' are a match for most popular emo rockers or cult power-poppers. Intriguing signs of maturity also crop up in the album's second half."

Florida's *Sun-Sentinel* observed, "What the Jonas Brothers accomplish on their third album is nearly impossible: Tweaking their songs enough to sound like upstanding pop-rock adults without losing the signature style that won them millions of Disney-loving fans in the first place." Michigan's *Detroit News* added that the disc is "top shelf power pop, and is bursting at the seams with restless energy, youthful exuberance and big

power chords. It's far from a swan song — if anything, it's a sign this young band could have the goods to transcend its made-for-TV background and earn a legitimate career crafting catchy three-minute pop songs for some time to come . . . Teen pop can be soulless, corporate drivel, but there are occasions where it is able to break through the clutter, and this is one of them."

Nick and Joe on the set of "Lovebug" with actress Camilla Belle (*10,000 BC*).

Once *A Little Bit Longer* was recorded, it was time for the Jonas Brothers to work on music videos to accompany the release of the album's singles. Directed by Brendan Malloy and Tim Wheeler, "Burnin' Up" was the biggest production for a Jonas Brothers video to date. Each Jonas has his own plot-line — Nick was a James Bond–type with Selena Gomez guest-starring as the Bond girl; Joe chased down criminals *Miami Vice* style with Big Rob and Kevin busted out his kung fu moves with David Carradine. The video premiered in June after *Camp Rock* on the Disney Channel. In September, the boys were back at it, hitting the set of "Lovebug" in pure 1940s style. The video, directed by Philip Andelman, told the story of a young couple finding out the husband has to go to war.

Never ones to rest on their laurels, shortly after the album's release, Kevin, Nick and Joe got right back to writing and laying down tracks for disc number four.

Chapter 20

Forever Jonas

Life for the Jonas Brothers isn't only about writing and performing their music, acting, touring the world and making appearances at events. Despite their insanely packed schedule, Kevin, Joe and Nick have always made time for two things they hold very close to their hearts: giving back to those less fortunate and showing their fans how much they appreciate their undying support.

Back when Nick was a kid working in New York for his Broadway performances, he was moved seeing a homeless family on the street and wanted to find a way to help them. With his dad's help, he started the Nicholas Jonas Change for the Children Foundation in 2002. The foundation focused on helping poor, homeless or terminally ill children.

When Joe and Kevin joined Nick in the music world, they wanted to give something back too. So the brothers turned Nick's charity into the Change for the Children Foundation (www.changeforthechildren.org). To define its mission, the JoBros wrote: "We started the Change for the Children Foundation to support programs that motivate and inspire children to face adversity with confidence, determination and a will to

Kevin, Joe and Nick visit with patients at St. Jude's Children's Research Hospital.

succeed. And we think the best people to help children are their peers — kids helping other kids who are a little less fortunate." The brothers gave the charity a big kick-start, donating 10% of their $12 million revenue from 2007.

Change for the Children supports five charities and allows donors to select their charity, and the brothers encourage, "YOU Decide. YOU Donate." The charities are:

▨ Nothing But Nets — a grassroots charity that seeks to reduce malaria by providing mosquito bed nets for children in Africa.

▨ American Diabetes Association Diabetes Camp — a charitable project that allows over 10,000 children with diabetes to go to camp each year.

▨ St. Jude's Children's Research Hospital — a hospital known for its groundbreaking research and its dedication to ensuring all patients get the best care possible, regardless of their medical insurance.

▨ Children's Hospital Los Angeles — a hospital with a Comprehensive Childhood Diabetes Care Center, helping children with diabetes lead regular lives.

▨ Summer Stars Camp for the Performing Arts — a charity that allows economically

The Jonas Brothers arrive at Concert of Hope, a benefit for cancer research and treatment programs at City of Hope.

disadvantaged kids between the ages of 12 and 15 to develop their skills and pursue their dreams at performing arts camp.

Since Nick was diagnosed with diabetes, the brothers were also inspired to start the D-VISION campaign. When fans buy special JoBros merchandise, a portion of the proceeds is donated to the Change for the Children Foundation. In August 2008 Nick also agreed to be a "diabetes ambassador" for Bayer Aspirin. With his Bayer campaign, Nick is promoting "Simple Wins" — the little things that make a difference when managing a disease like diabetes. As they continue to play charity concerts and donate signed guitars and merchandise, the Jonas Brothers have proven time and time again that they are rock stars with heart.

This earnestness to give back to the community and to spread the wealth that they have been so fortunate to earn at such

> **We think the best people to help children are their peers — kids helping other kids who are a little less fortunate.**

a young age is part of what makes the fans of the Jonas Brothers love them so much. Since the early days of the Jonas Brothers, their fans have shown a special kind of loyalty to the boys, one that goes beyond the usual enthusiasm for the latest hot performer. It even has its own nickname within the fandom, OJD or Obsessive Jonas Disorder. In addition to joining the official Jonas Brothers fan club, Team Jonas, fans show their mad love by requesting JoBros songs and videos, voting for them in online polls and for awards, commenting on critiques of the band online, showing up in the thousands for any public appearance, buying concert tickets and albums and merchandise and generally spreading the word about the awesomeness that is the brothers Jonas. And the boys know how lucky they are to have such a dedicated fan base and make sure they *always* keep in touch: through various social networking sites, with their video and blog posts, with contests, meet and greets and off-the-wall original ideas like having fans sign their tour bus.

The growing number of Jonas fans believe in the brothers, whose legend, it would seem, will continue to grow as time goes on and Kevin, Joe and Nick are able to spread their music around the globe, evolving as musicians and bringing their fans along for the journey.

"Everything that's happened is the best thing that has ever happened to me," enthused Kevin. "It's one of the most crazy and most fun lives ever. I have a blast every single day. If I wasn't doing this, I'd probably be working at Starbucks, so the fact that I get to travel around on a tour bus all around the country is pretty awesome."

"Life is probably about as insane as it could ever be right now," added Joe. "We are running all over the place, but this is all very exciting to us."

Nick admitted, "We just really enjoy it. A lot of kids may wish for what we have, but the fact that we're able to have it is something that we're just so grateful about. It's just so amazing for all of us. I think we're just having a great time and living the dream."

And helping them to maintain and be true to that dream are the people that they surround themselves with on a daily basis. Said Kevin, "We keep it a very tight-knit group. Our father's our co-manager. Our road manager is our uncle. They're both pastors and they can both minister to us on the road. It's a really great thing to know that we have a tight and close group of people with us."

It's one of the most crazy and most fun lives ever. I have a blast every single day.

The one big question that remains is *why* Kevin, Joe and Nick have so touched a chord with people. It's Kevin's opinion that they represent something that whole families can connect with, "from little kids to the teenage daughters and even the guys. Even the parents. They all enjoy the music, so they can go see [us] together, which is something that hasn't happened in a long time."

"Probably the last time that happened was with *NSync," Nick suggested, to which Joe added, "That's kind of what we're discovering and it's pretty incredible."

As to how someone can adjust themselves to this kind of success achieved so quickly, Joe said matter of factly, "If it's a change that you like, it's something you can deal with." As far as Kevin is concerned, the best career advice they've received was at the outset of their careers when they were an aspiring, struggling opening act. "It came from Nick Carter from the Backstreet Boys," he reflected. "He said to us, 'Watch the mistakes of the people you admire most, and don't make those same mistakes. Be true to yourself.'"

Chapter 21

That's Just the Way They Roll

THE JONAS BROTHERS NEWS DIARY

A MONTH-BY-MONTH LOOK
AT THE BAND'S FIRST FOUR YEARS

Early 2005

Columbia Records president Steve Greenberg signed the Jonas Brothers after hearing the Jonas-penned "Please Be Mine" off Nick's solo album. "We knew we could do this," said Kevin to the *New Haven Register*, "The pieces started falling into place." Nick was equally excited about the record deal. "We're so blessed to have this opportunity to be signed to Columbia. It's awesome. We're ready for the big stuff and super excited."

May 2005

A solo song by Nick, "Crazy Kinda Crush on You," appears on the soundtrack to *Darcy's Wild Life*.

Summer 2005

The boys joined Jesse McCartney, The Click Five and the Backstreet Boys on their tours as the opening act. Thousands of fans were introduced to the Jonas Brothers' music in advance of their debut album's release.

Fall 2005

The Jonas Brothers embarked on a promotional tour. "We're having a blast," said Nick at the time. "We're going to schools every morning and playing shows with The Veronicas. Then we go to the venue for the night's show." Part of the tour was in service of a good cause: anti-drug promotion in schools. "We were totally for it, because we definitely want to make a difference," Joe said. "We totally wanted to be a good influence."

November 2005

After noticing all the telltale signs, Nick was diagnosed with type 1 diabetes. Looking

The first CD Joe ever bought was Britney's debut album and he finally got the chance to tell her at the 2008 VMAs. Kevin is also a fan, telling the media, "A duet with Britney one day would be amazing."

The Jonas Brothers arrive at the 2006 Teen Choice Awards on August 20.

back in 2008, Kevin recalled how strong the youngest Jonas brother was during this difficult time, "I remember sitting down with [Frankie] and said, 'Nick is in the hospital, and he'll be home in a couple of days.' He hugged us and he said, 'He'll be OK.'"

December 2005
🌿 The Jonas Brothers were a surprise opening act for 10 shows on The Cheetah Girls' Cheetah-licious Christmas Tour.
🌿 On December 27, the Jonas Brothers released their very first single, "Mandy."

January 2006
🌼 Kevin, Joe and Nick started 2006 with more live performances. Kicking off their American Club Tour on the 28th in Sacramento, California, the Jonas Brothers toured until March 3 in Orlando, Florida.

February 2006
🦌 The first video for "Mandy" debuted on *TRL* on the 22nd. "We shot three music videos for the same song and are debuting each one at a separate time," Kevin told MTV.com. "The first one was on the [*TRL*] countdown for the entire time. And then we went for the second one. It's still on. And for the third one, we're going back to perform, so we're so excited."
🦌 The JoBros' song "Time for Me to Fly" was released as part of the *Aquamarine* soundtrack.

≁ Originally due out in February, *It's About Time* was pushed back at the label's request that the band add another "lead single" to the album.

March 2006

The *Zoey 101: Spring Break-Up* soundtrack featured "Mandy," the Jonas Brothers' first hit song.

April 2006

For the *DisneyMania 4* album, the JoBros covered "Yo Ho (A Pirate's Life for Me)" from *Pirates of the Caribbean*.

June 2006

For its second season, the Disney Channel show *American Dragon: Jake Long* featured the Jonas Brothers performing its theme song, "The Chosen One."

Summer 2006

≁ The JoBros hit the road again, touring with Aly & AJ.

August 2006

It was about time! On August 8, Columbia finally released *It's About Time*, the debut record from the Jonas Brothers. The sound of the Jonas Brothers debut, as

famously described by Kevin, is "music on Red Bull."

October 2006

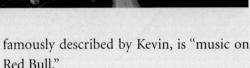 "Joy to the World (A Christmas Prayer)," Nick's single from 2004, was re-released on October 3 as part of *Joy to the World: The Ultimate Christmas Collection.*

For *The Little Mermaid* special two-disc soundtrack, the Jonas Brothers covered "Poor Unfortunate Souls" and filmed a video for the track.

Early 2007

The video for the second single from *It's About Time* — "Year 3000" — debuted on the Disney Channel and made some waves on Radio Disney.

The Jonas Brothers were released from their contract with Columbia Records.

February 2007

Hollywood Records scooped up the JoBros, signing them to a record deal. "Boys identify with them, and girls love them because they're cute," Radio Disney executive Jill Casagrande told the Associated Press at the time of their signing.

The Jonas Brothers sign their first endorsement deal with Baby Bottle Pop, singing the jingle and appearing in advertisements.

March 2007

The Jonas Brothers continued to contribute songs to soundtrack albums with

"Kids of the Future" appearing on the *Meet the Robinsons* soundtrack.

🐾 *The Jungle Book*'s "I Wanna Be Like You" as performed by the brothers Jonas was featured on *DisneyMania 5*.

April 2007

🎖 Kevin, Joe and Nick sang the national anthem at the White House for the annual Easter Egg Roll on April 9.

🎖 Now part of the Disney family, the JoBros taped a performance at the second annual Disney Channel Games, held at the Wide World of Sports complex in Lake Buena Vista, Florida, along with labelmates Miley Cyrus and The Cheetah Girls.

🎖 Not long thereafter they were back in home state New Jersey, performing at the Bamboozle Festival 2007, an annual event devoted to emo, punk, hardcore and indie music held at the Meadowlands in New Jersey.

🎖 On the 13th, the Jonas Brothers were back in familiar territory: opening for Jesse McCartney in Boca Raton, Florida. But this time the boys were arguably more popular than the headlining act.

May 2007

🐾 *Johnny Kapahala: Back on Board* premiered on the Disney Channel on the 18th and Jonas Brothers fans tuned in; the movie

featured the soon-to-be-hit song "Hold On."

꠸ Kevin, Joe and Nick filmed an episode of *Hannah Montana*, "Me and Mr. Jonas and Mr. Jonas and Mr. Jonas," from the 14th to 18th.

꠸ A mark of the Jonas Brothers climbing success? The trio was featured on *CosmoGirl*'s Hot 100 list.

June 2007

꘎ The buzz for their sophomore album heightened when tickets to the Jonas Brothers' CD release party in New York City sold out in 15 minutes. The response was so overwhelming that a second date was added.

꘎ In an interview with *People* magazine, Billy Ray Cyrus fueled rumors that Nick and Miley Cyrus were dating but only going on "group dates."

꘎ On June 17, the boys headlined the Target Children's Day and Fireworks at New York's South Street Seaport.

꘎ The Jonas Brothers boarded the *Queen Mary* in Long Beach, California, on the 18th to film the video for "S.O.S."

꘎ The day after filming their video, the JoBros performed at the Alameda California Fair, where they absolutely thrilled their gathered fans. *Inside Bay Area* noted, "Toward the end of their set, the Jonas Brothers had the crowd following their every command — whether it was to jump, wave arms or sing along."

꘎ The guys' dedication to charity work continued with their participation in the Children's Miracle Network's 25th Anniversary Celebration telethon, raising money for the underprivileged.

꘎ On the 27th, Kevin, Nick and Joe were back at the White House for the Celebrating Women in Sports Tee-Ball game. Once again, they performed the national anthem as well as some of their own songs at a post-game reception.

꘎ The boys kicked off their Prom Tour (also called the Marvelous Party Tour) at the end of the month, and it continued all the way into October.

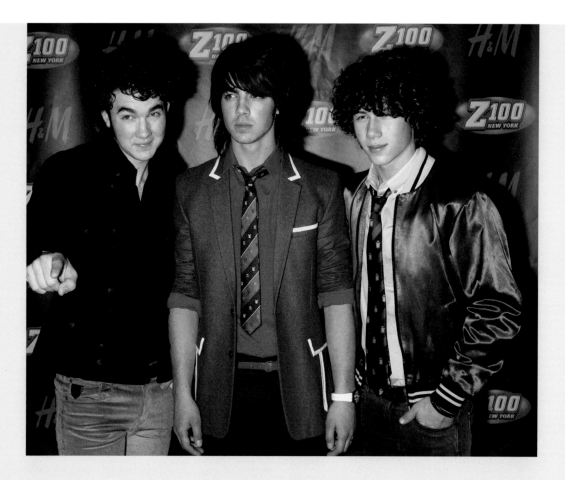

July 2007

～ Nick, Joe and Kevin joined Kenny Loggins, REO Speedwagon and Joan Jett, among others, at the annual San Diego Fair.

～ On the 24th, the first single from *Jonas Brothers*, "Hold On," was released.

August 2007

⊠ The album's second single, "S.O.S.," was released and its video debuted on August 3 on Disney Channel.

⊠ *Jonas Brothers* was released on the 7th and hit #5 on the *Billboard* Hot 200.

⊠ On August 17, the Jonas episode of *Hannah Montana* debuted right after the premiere of *High School Musical 2*.

⊠ The Miss Teen USA pageant was graced with a performance by the brothers Jonas on the 24th.

⊠ Taped back in April, the Disney Channel Games performance aired on the 25th of an already Jonas-filled month.

⊠ At the Teen Choice Awards on the 26th, Kevin, Joe and Nick joined Miley Cyrus to present an award and announced that they would be touring together.

October 2007

～ The *Disney Holiday Album 2007*, released on the 16th, featured "Girl of My Dreams," by the Jonas Brothers.

Kevin, Joe and Nick perform at the Walt Disney World Christmas Day Parade, filmed on December 1, 2007.

The Best of Both Worlds tour began on the 18th to a sold-out St. Louis crowd.

The deluxe edition of *Jonas Brothers* was released on the 30th, featuring a bonus DVD with music videos for "Year 3000," "S.O.S." and "Hold On" as well as live performance videos and other JoBros goodies.

November 2007

The Jonas Brothers hit the stage at the American Music Awards to perform "S.O.S." Joe accidentally tripped over a shattered glass frame used to introduce them, and ended up on his knees. Ever the trooper, and not seriously injured, he pushed on through his performance.

On the 22nd, Kevin, Nick and Joe joined other celebrities in the Macy's Thanksgiving Day parade.

December 2007

The Jonas Brothers ended a landmark year by performing "Hold On" and "S.O.S." on *Dick Clark's New Year's Rockin Eve*.

January 2008

🐚 Not long after wrapping up the Best of Both Worlds tour, the Look Me in the Eyes tour started on the 31st. The Jonas Brothers performed songs from their upcoming album, *A Little Bit Longer*.

🐚 The Jonas Brothers inked a landmark deal with Live Nation, which was called the first of its kind for an up-and-coming group by *Billboard*. The multimillion-dollar agreement committed the boys to 140 shows over two years.

March 2008

🏵 The Jonas Brothers returned to the White House for the Easter Egg Roll, performing the national anthem.

🏵 Performing "When You Look Me in the Eyes" as well as a cover of "Take on Me," the Jonas Brothers appeared on *Dancing With the Stars* on the 25th.

🏵 On the 29th, the boys took home the Kids' Choice Award for Best Musical Group.

🏵 All a part of the jam-packed Jonas life: a quick jet flight over to England so the boys could perform for the bigwigs at Universal

Kevin and Joe go for a spin on a *Toy Story* ride at Disney's Hollywood Studios theme park. The boys were there to participate in the Disney Channel Games.

Records, the new international distributors for Hollywood Records. "We do lead a pretty crazy life," said Kevin. "We were in one place, we had a day off and flew to London for 12 hours, and then we had to come back home to do another show."

April 2008

⬚ Kevin, Joe and Nick filmed a video for the *Idol Gives Back* special on the 9th, encouraging viewers to donate money for children in need in the U.S. and around the world.

⬚ On April 24, the Jonas Brothers appeared as guests on *Oprah* after fans barraged the show with pleas to have them on, making the boys the most requested guests of the year.

⬚ The Jonas Brothers joined a host of other celebrities at the annual White House Correspondents Dinner on the 26th. "We hear we're sitting with Martha Stewart,"

hit show. Nick revealed, "When we heard [we would be on the show], we were freaking out. We were in the studio, actually, working with Demi Lovato — we're co-producing her record — and they told us, and we were like, 'Awesome!'"

June 2008

🌿 An exciting month for Jonas Brothers fans: the soundtrack to *Camp Rock* was released days before the movie's premiere, on the 17th.

🌿 On the 20th, *Camp Rock* premiered on the Disney Channel featuring the Jonas Brothers as the band Connect 3.

🌿 In a special release structure, iTunes announced it would be releasing four songs from the upcoming JoBros album, one about every two weeks. The first was the debut single, "Burnin' Up," on the 24th.

July 2008

➴ On July 4th in Toronto, Kevin, Nick and Joe launched their North American Burning Up tour to a sold-out audience.

➴ A production crew filmed two shows on the Burning Up tour (July 13 and July 14 in Anaheim, California) for a 3D movie similar to the hit *Hannah Montana & Miley Cyrus: Best of Both Worlds Concert*.

➴ iTunes continued to release songs from *A Little Bit Longer*: on the 15th, "Pushin' Me Away" and on the 29th, "Tonight." The boys made history by being the first to have three consecutive singles sell over 100,000 in digital downloads.

Kevin told People.com before the event. "That will be really cool. Hopefully by the end of the night, she'll say we have good table manners."

May 2008

〰 The JoBros joined Avril Lavigne on her Best Damn Tour in Europe from May to late June.

〰 Their Disney Channel series *Jonas Brothers: Living the Dream* premiered on May 16.

〰 Appearing on *American Idol*'s finale, the Jonases were excited to be a part of the

◌ A true mark of "making it": the boys were on the cover of *Rolling Stone* magazine for its July issue.

◌ Rumors that Nick was dating Selena Gomez were fueled when they each shared *very* similar stories about a first kiss with a current crush to different magazines.

August 2008

❋ *Variety* announced the release date for the Jonas Brothers 3D concert film: February 27, 2009.

❋ Performing "Burnin' Up," the Jonas Brothers made a special outdoor appearance on *The Tonight Show with Jay Leno*.

❋ "A Little Bit Longer" made its debut on iTunes on the 5th.

Held aloft by the screams of their fans (and wires), the Jonas Brothers fly over the audience at the Teen Choice Awards.

It was Jonas Brothers fan week on *TRL* leading up to the release of *A Little Bit Longer*.

The long-awaited day arrived: on August 12, the Jonas Brothers released their third album, *A Little Bit Longer*.

In mid-August, Kevin, Nick and Joe were spotted filming scenes for their 3D movie in Central Park along with Joe's rumored girlfriend, Taylor Swift.

The JoBros donated the clothing worn on the cover of *A Little Bit Longer* to the Right Here! Right Now! exhibit at the Rock and Roll Hall of Fame in Cleveland.

Bayer Diabetes Care partnered with Nick to promote diabetes management for young people, calling him a "diabetes ambassador."

"Burnin' Up" received the first MTV VMA nomination for the Jonas Brothers in the Best Pop category.

The Jonas Brothers swept the 2008

Double the Jonas! Kevin, Joe and Nick pose by their wax figures at Madame Tussauds in Washington.

Teen Choice Awards winning six awards: Choice Music Single, Breakout Group, Music Love Song, Summer Song, Male Hottie and Red Carpet Fashion Icon Male.

Miley Cyrus broke the silence about her relationship with Nick in *Seventeen* saying, "Nick and I loved each other. We still do, but we were in love with each other. For two years he was basically my 24/7. But it was really hard to keep it from people."

September 2008

Nominees at the VMAS, the Jonas Brothers also performed their second single, "Lovebug" on the set of Chris's brownstone house from *Everybody Hates Chris*. On performing at the VMAS, the brothers said in a press release, "This is an awesome opportunity. We have grown up watching all the amazing and iconic performances on the VMAS. It is an honor to be a part of something so incredible."

In mid-September, the boys were back in front of the cameras filming the video for "Lovebug."

For Nick's 16th birthday, the Jonas Brothers rented out L.A.'s Dodger Stadium to play baseball with their friends. Nick's favorite birthday gift? A dog named Elvis, named after both Elvis Presley and Elvis Costello.

Camp Rock premiered in the U.K. on the 19th and a special called *Jonas Brothers: Live in London* aired, which was filmed during their tour with Avril.

On the 23rd, Demi Lovato's album *Don't Forget* was released, featuring a duet with the Jonas Brothers as well as several songs they helped compose.

Back on *Dancing with the Stars* on the 24th, the Jonas Brothers performed "Lovebug" and Joe debuted his tap dancing skills with pros Mark Ballas and Derek Hough. "Joe wasn't sure that he wanted to do the little 'tap' thing with us," Hough told People.com. "He was like, 'I'm not sure I want to dance next to you guys, because you guys are professional dancers.' But we were like, 'C'mon, man! Let's just go out there, tap our feet a little bit, and have some fun.' We taught him a little 'tap-tap-step,' and that was it. I thought he did an amazing job."

The Jonas Brothers began filming their long awaited Disney series, *JONAS*. The boys reported, "It's also been so exciting being onset for the first week of our new Disney Show, JONAS. We've been doing lots of fittings, table reads and rehearsals getting ready for our first week of TAPING next week. There will be lots of 'surprise' guests and we are just so excited about it and hope you are too!"

October 2008

The Jonas Brothers performed in a charity concert on 17th in Las Vegas hosted by Justin Timberlake with Leona Lewis, 50 Cent and Rihanna also performing. The show was a benefit for the Shriners Hospitals for Children.

In addition to their upcoming 3D concert movie, it was announced that the Jonas Brothers would be in the film adaptation of the bestselling book series *Walter the Farting Dog*, along with little bro Frankie.

Kevin and former Wychoff, New Jersey, neighbor Danielle Deleasa began spending time in public together as a couple. Danielle was in an episode of *Living the Dream* and fans had guessed she was Kevin's girlfriend, but paparazzi photos confirmed the relationship.

November 2008

Kevin had a milestone birthday on the 5th, turning 21 on the set of *JONAS* where, he revealed on MySpace, "everyone showed up at the set and sang Happy Birthday."

The JoBros were up for Best New Act at the 2008 MTV Europe Video Awards, but lost to the show's host Katy Perry.

Taylor Swift, while promoting her album *Fearless*, was asked about her relationship

with Joe Jonas and revealed that they had dated and he had broken up with her over the phone. Her song "Forever and Always" was written about their failing romance. Rumored to have moved on with Camilla Belle, who starred in the "Lovebug" video, Joe responded on the JoBros' MySpace blog, giving his side of the story.

The Disney Book Group published *Burning Up: On Tour with the Jonas Brothers* on the 18th, an exclusive behind-the-scenes book sharing never-before-seen photos and commentary from the boys,

giving fans a glimpse backstage on the Burning Up tour. The boys launched the book in New York City and over 500 fans camped out in a line-up for days to get the chance to meet their idols.

The Jonas Brothers were back at the American Music Awards on the 23rd to perform "Tonight." The boys won the T-Mobile Breakthrough Artist Award.

The JoBros performed "Tonight," "Lovebug," and "Burnin' Up" on Thanksgiving Day during halftime of the Dallas Cowboys v. Seattle Seahawks football game.

December 2008

🜲 Kevin, Joe and Nick joined Jamie Foxx, Tony Bennett, Harry Connick Jr., Rosie O'Donnell, Faith Hill and others for the annual tree-lighting ceremony in Rockefeller Center on the 3rd.

🜲 One of many "best of the year" lists to include Kevin, Joe and Nick, *Forbes* named the Jonas Brothers Breakout Stars of 2008.

🜲 The Jonas Brothers were nominated in the Best New Artist category for the 51st Annual Grammy Awards, to be handed out on February 8, 2009.

🜲 Bringing an already amazing 2008 to a close, the brothers returned to Dick Clark's *New Year's Rockin' Eve* for one final performance of the year.

Also available from ECW Press

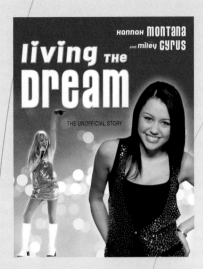

Living the Dream
Hannah Montana and Miley Cyrus
The Unofficial Story

All in This Together
The Unofficial Story of
High School Musical

Get the scoop on the girl behind that world-famous smile in *Living the Dream*, the first backstage look at Miley Cyrus and *Hannah Montana*. From Tennessean cheerleader to Oscar presenter, Miley's story is all captured here: her life before *Hannah*, her albums (and Hannah's too), the Best of Both Worlds tour, the upcoming *Hannah Montana* movie, and a month-by-month look at Miley's meteoric rise to superstardom. Featuring tons of full-color photos of Miley and her friends and family (some never published before!), plus bios of Billy Ray Cyrus ("Robby Ray"), Jason Earles ("Jackson"), Emily Osment ("Lilly"), Mitchel Musso ("Oliver") and more, *Living the Dream* also includes a *Hannah Montana* episode guide full of fun facts and bloopers! Sweet niblets!

You've memorized the lyrics and know all the dance moves. Time to find out the story behind the scenes of *High School Musical*! The little movie about breaking free from stereotypes and being true to yourself turned into an explosive event. *All in This Together* offers the first look at how the movie got made, bios of the six stars — Zac Efron (Troy), Vanessa Hudgens (Gabriella), Ashley Tisdale (Sharpay), Corbin Bleu (Chad), Monique Coleman (Taylor) and Lucas Grabeel (Ryan) — an exciting look at their solo careers plus dozens of full color never-before-seen photos of the cast. If you're a fan of *High School Musical*, this is the book you've been looking for!

Visit **ecwpress.com** for an announcement about our upcoming book on
Demi Lovato and Selena Gomez!